102 DON'TS BEFORE YOU SAY "I Do"

THE SOMEWHAT COMPLETE GUIDE TO
WEDDING MISHAPS

"WE LAUGHED OUT LOUD OVER AND OVER READING THIS BOOK.
IT DEFINITELY MADE PLANNING OUR WEDDING A LOT MORE ENJOYABLE!"

JASON & ABBIE ROTELLO, MARRIED JULY 2006

"A MUST READ FOR ANYONE WHO IS PLANNING
A WEDDING AND NEEDS A GOOD LAUGH!"

TOM & TRISH LEWIS, MARRIED JULY 2007

"THE ILLUSTRATIONS ARE HILARIOUS.
THIS BOOK IS A GREAT GIFT FOR THE NEWLY ENGAGED!"

MARCUS & JONNA LESHOCK, MARRIED SEPTEMBER 2007

DON'T FORGET TO VISIT US ONLINE AT WEDDINGMISHAPS.COM

Copyright © 2009 by SolidLine Media, a division of KV Media Group, Inc.

Written by Gregory Vass & Michael Kromm
Illustrations by Mike Petrik

All rights reserved. No part of this book may be reproduced, stored, or transmitted by any means—whether auditory, graphic, mechanical, or electronic—without written permission of both publisher and author, except in the case of brief excerpts used in critical articles and reviews. Unauthorized reproduction of any part of this book is illegal and is punishable by law.

ISBN: 978-0-578-02687-9

For Our Kids

Introduction

Welcome to our wide world of wedding faults and mishaps—we're glad you're here. You are, however, already probably asking yourself: "What gives these two lifelong buddies the right to construe a book about wedding "don'ts" anyway"? Now that is a good question. And here is the answer. For four years, we ran a rather successful wedding DJ entertainment company in Chicago called Platinum Sounds. We had tons of fun with it and met a number of truly great people. So why did we give it up you ask? Well, have you ever been to thirty-eight weddings in a row? Try doing it for four years straight. It was just time to hang up the polyester tuxedos and focus on our other prospering business. So we did. And that was that.

A year later, however, a certain list surfaced while organizing some files in our downtown Chicago office. The list was one that we built over our years as wedding entertainers (although we probably entertained ourselves more than anyone else). Anyway, this list was of everything horrible and stupid we saw during the 124 weddings at which we entertained. So after a bit of discussion and about four dirty martinis, we decided to write a book. So we did. And that was that.

But wait. Why write a book about wedding don'ts? Listen, there are so many books and resources out there about what you should do and how it should be done that we figured it's time to get critical. It's time to expose the stupidity and laziness in the wedding industry. What you will read in this book all actually happened, believe it or not. And it happened over and over and over again. Some things are more believable than others, but you get the point. Why did it happen? Well, some things are just bad ideas, and others are just really bad ideas. The cold hard truth is that most people don't like to go to weddings. Why? What we hear is because every wedding is so predictable, so standard. And it's not the standard fun things that people hate—it's the standard not fun things—the things you are about to read in this well-crafted masterpiece, or poorly written bathroom book, depending on your tastes. Of course, you have to follow a certain chronological order of events during your wedding day, but you do not have to do everything by the book. After all, there is no book on your wedding—not yet at least. Don't be manipulated by your vendors or possessive family and friends. Do whatever you want at your wedding—except, of course, what we are about to tell you not to do. The moral of our story is simple: take control of your wedding by not allowing anyone to take control of you.

So, enjoy our book, take our reasons for what they are, and have an awesome wedding day. And if you have any questions during your planning, you can always send us an e-mail online at www.weddingmishaps.com. Depending on how sales are going, we will either be there, or not be there, to respond. You can even send us any wedding "don'ts" that you may have seen over the years right from our Web site. You never know, we might just even add 'em into the second version of our book. You can also buy a coffee mug or a hat that you will never wear.

And that's that. Good story.

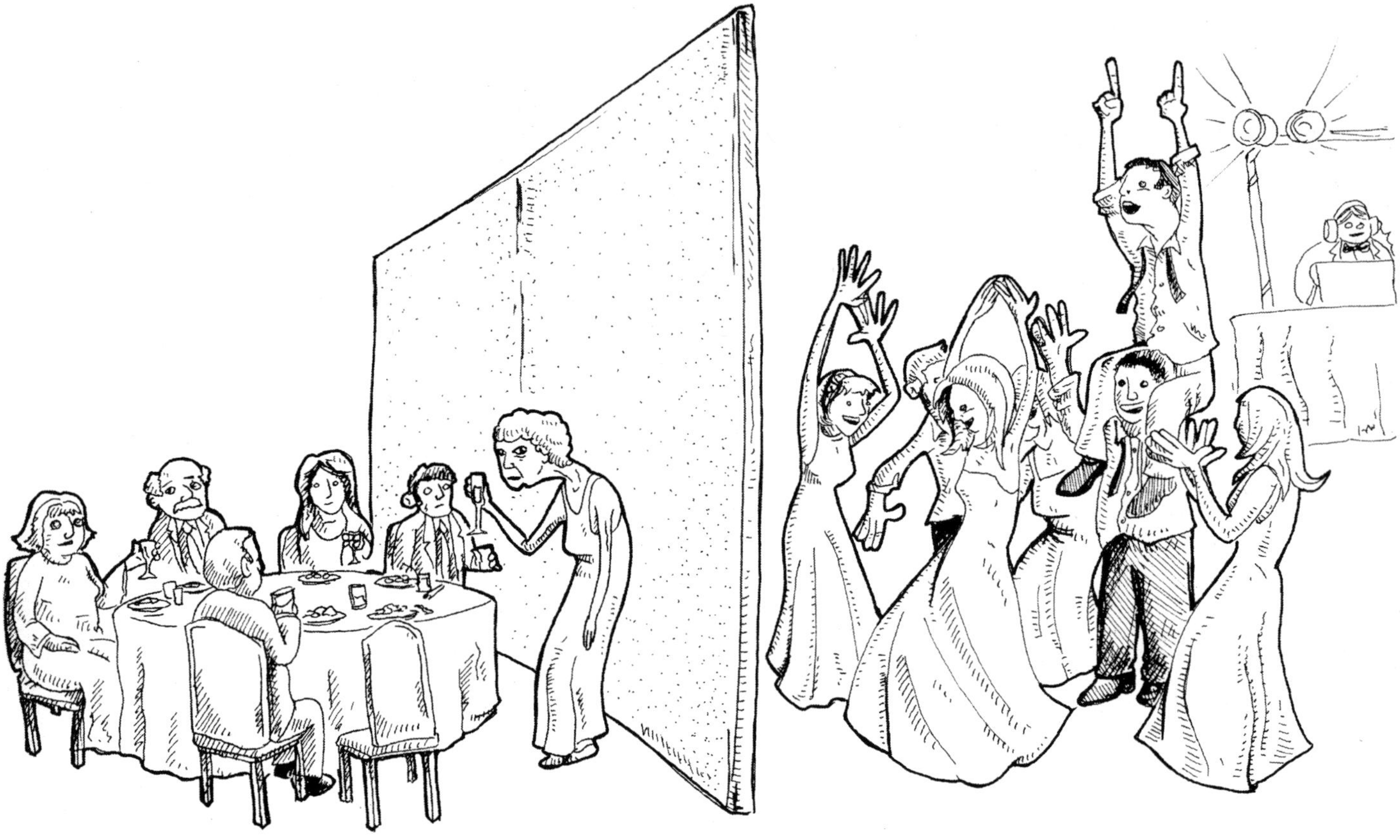

1

DON'T rent a room with a divider wall

Unless you want to participate in two, or maybe three, weddings at once, having a room with a divider wall is not a good idea. Move on to another banquet hall—there are plenty more. No matter what the banquet coordinator says, you will hear the wedding next to you. But, really, when you think about it, there is nothing sweeter than hearing a muffled "Baby Got Back" during your grandmother's special toast, right? Wrong.

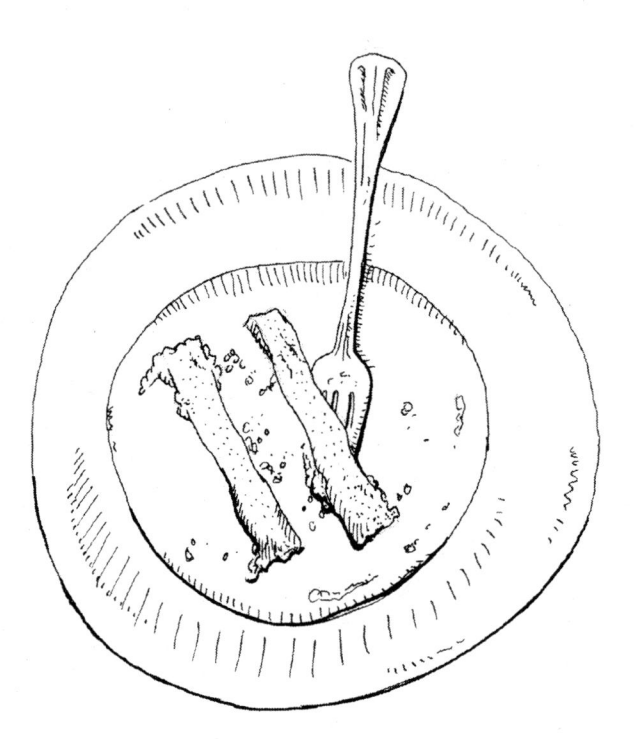

2

DON'T have fruit in your wedding cake

Listen, unless you want a lot of leftover cake, keep it simple. While your favorite dessert combo might be marble cake mixed with peaches and cream, most likely that is not the favorite of your guests. Fruit and dessert just simply do not always mix. Keeping your cake simple, cake and frosting for example, will result in empty plates. It is pretty amazing, however, to see the efforts guests have made to eat around fruit in wedding cake—with only a few crumbs and the inner strip of strawberry glazed apples left behind. Nasty.

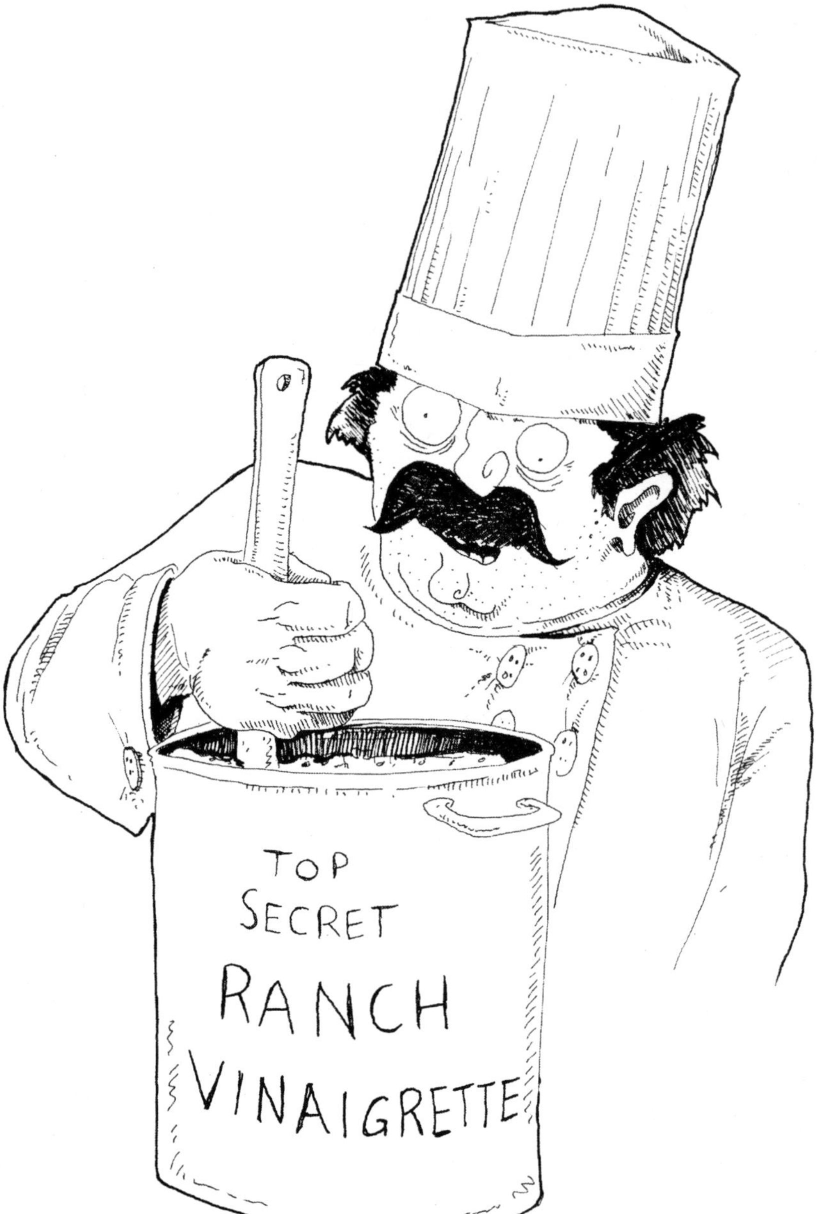
TOP
SECRET
RANCH
VINAIGRETTE

∽ 3 ∾

DON'T offer just one salad dressing selection

The last time we checked, there was no such dressing as a ranch vinaigrette. Unless you have this magic recipe tucked away ready to reveal at your wedding, we suggest you offer a selection. A minimum of two is suggested, but a ranch, a French, and a vinaigrette are best. Again, do not listen to your wedding coordinator here. It is more of a pain for the kitchen, but more of a service for your guests.

COUNTDOWN TO
MY WEDDING
3 7 2 DAYS
3
PAST DUE
DJ'S
CHURCHES
LIMO'S
GUEST LIST
BRIDE 2 BE

~ 4 ~

DON'T stress out over the small details too early

Think about how stressed out you are right now, a year before your wedding. Now, keep track of the details today and how they actually turn out on your wedding date. Everything will change—over and over again. We suggest you just relax instead of freaking out about how long the salad course will take. We hate to say something you have certainly heard before, but everything will all work out.

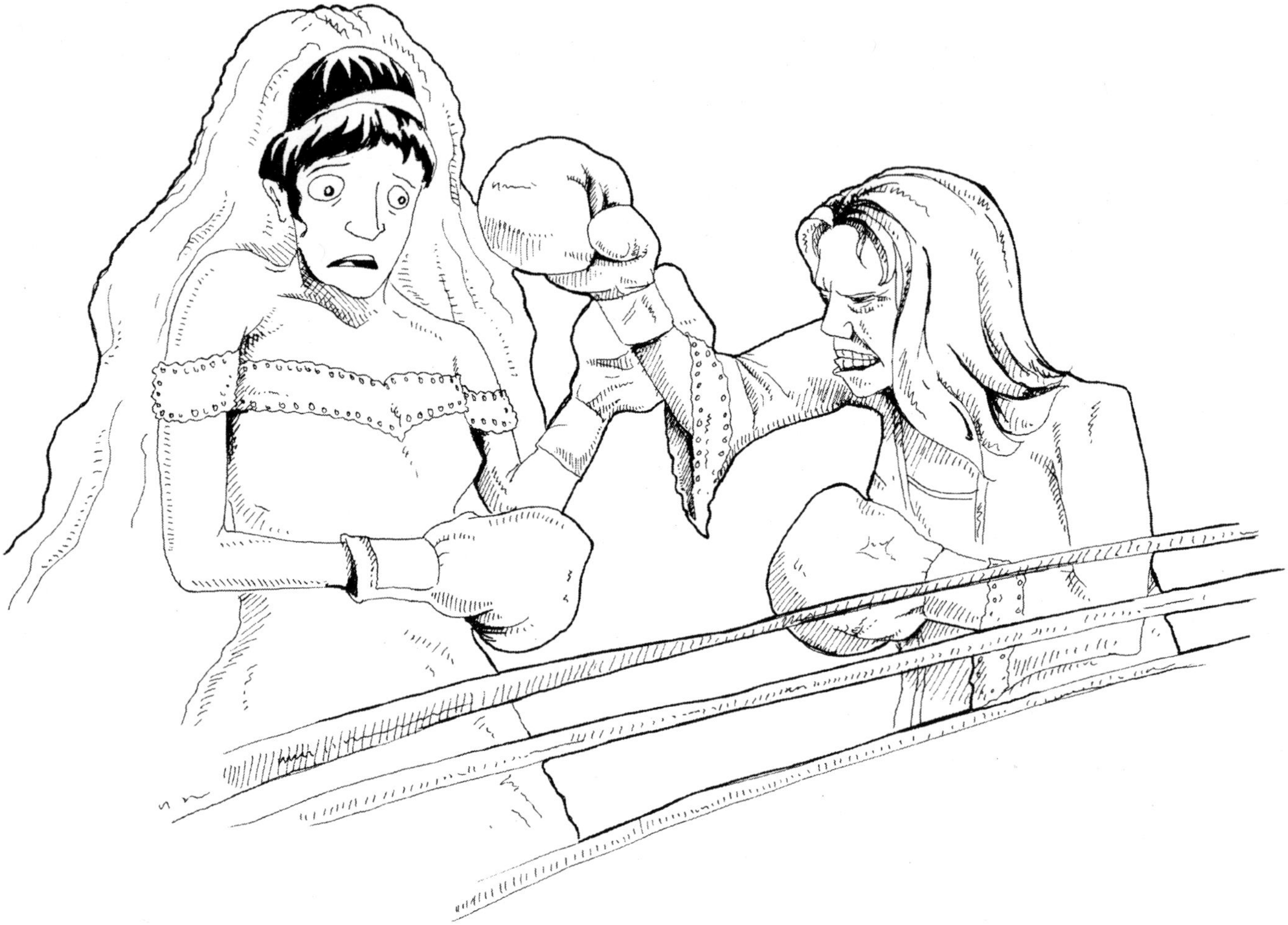

5

DON'T forget how your family used to be before wedding plans began

Of course you need to plan, but we have seen so many families torn apart from stress and anxiety about a wedding. Seriously, we have seen moms and brides not speaking because of disagreements and stress. It is so silly. Calm down. Relax. This is supposed to be a fun day. And it will be—maybe.

16

6

DON'T rent a room for 100 when you have 150 guests

So, you want to invite 50 people, and your parents want to invite 100? OK, that is a total of 150 guests. Now, the wedding coordinator says you can easily fit 150 into the only room they have available—the room for 100. This will work out just fine, right? No, no it won't. Sounds like it's time to find a new banquet hall. It is hard to gauge how many people can fit into a room when you are shopping around, but rest assured, a room that is too small equals a hot, claustrophobic, and miserable experience. Get a bigger room, not a smaller one. Otherwise, your best friends will be getting to know your Uncle Frank a little more intimately than you would ever want them to.

7

DON'T have your wedding on a Sunday

Unless it is for religious reasons, Sunday weddings are a waste of a potential great time—the weekend is over, and the work week is about to begin. Nobody wants to go to a party on a Sunday. Unless, of course, it is in late January and involves a big screen. Save up for the Saturday and get back the fun!

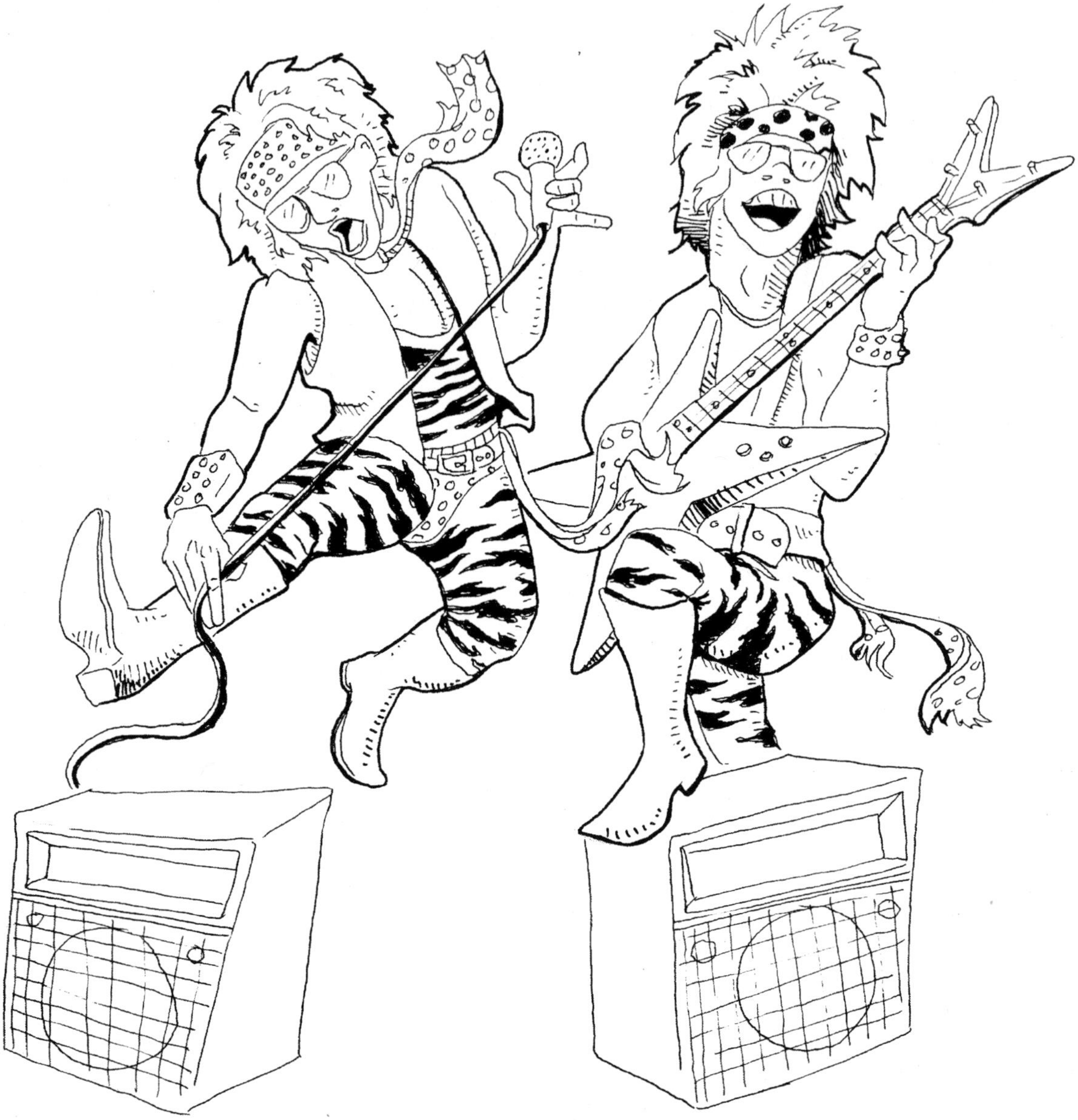

8

DON'T hire a band without a wide popular music selection

A band can be awesome if they are playing music that your guests enjoy and can dance to. But what happens when the band starts to play their "unique" and "original" songs? Well, most likely the bus to the hotel will end up departing earlier than expected. Good news for the hotel bar. Bad news for your party. Make sure the band sticks to popular party tunes.

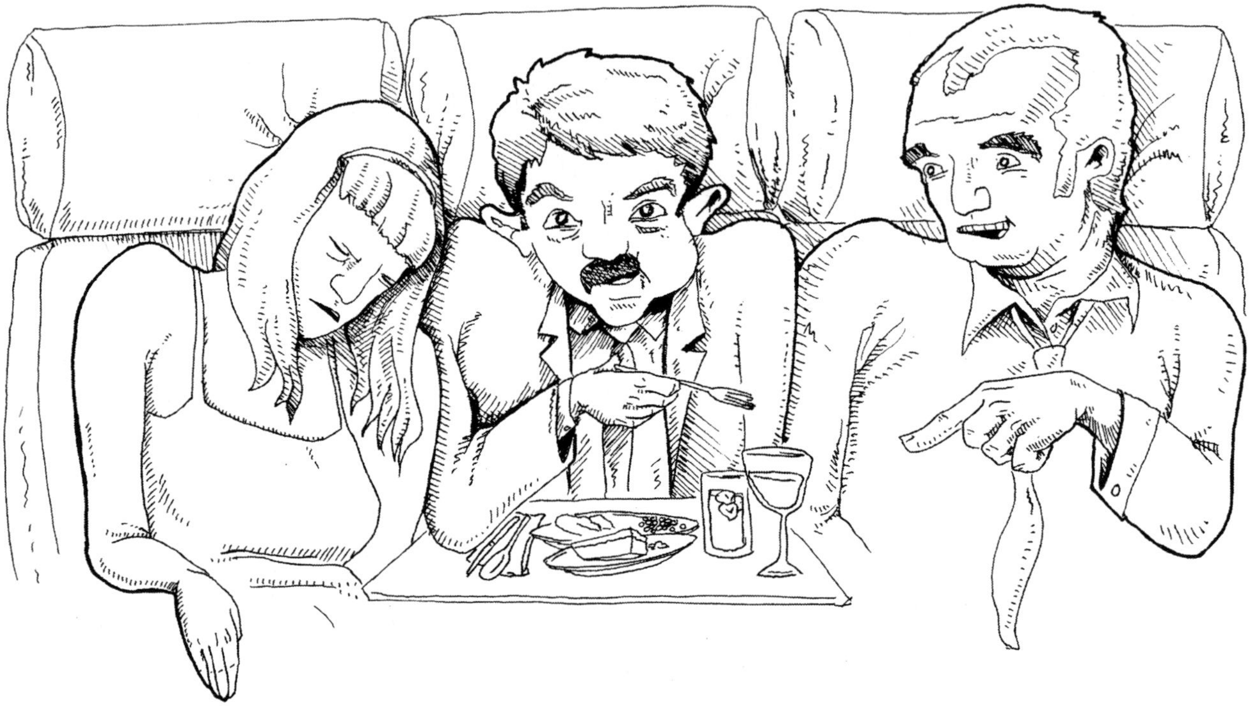

9

DON'T seat twelve guests around a table for eight

Have you ever eaten a five-course meal in the middle seat of an airplane? That should cover it for this one.

24

10

DON'T listen to the banquet coordinator

What are these guys talking about you ask? Have they gone mad this early in the book? No, in fact, we have not. It is true—you need your banquet coordinator to coordinate your reception. But the key word here is "your." It is your wedding, and you should be calling the shots on what you want, not on what is most convenient for the coordinator. That is really all it is for them—convenience. Banquet hall coordinators do this every weekend and sometimes several nights a week. Do you really think your wedding is special to them? We think not. While they are happy to have you spending money with their hall, what they really want is to make it as easy as possible on themselves without pissing you off. Keep this very true fact in mind when planning the details of your night. Do not skimp on something you are excited about just because the coordinator says it is not the "best idea." Please understand we are talking about banquet coordinators here, not wedding planners! Wedding planners actually help—after all, that's all they are getting paid for.

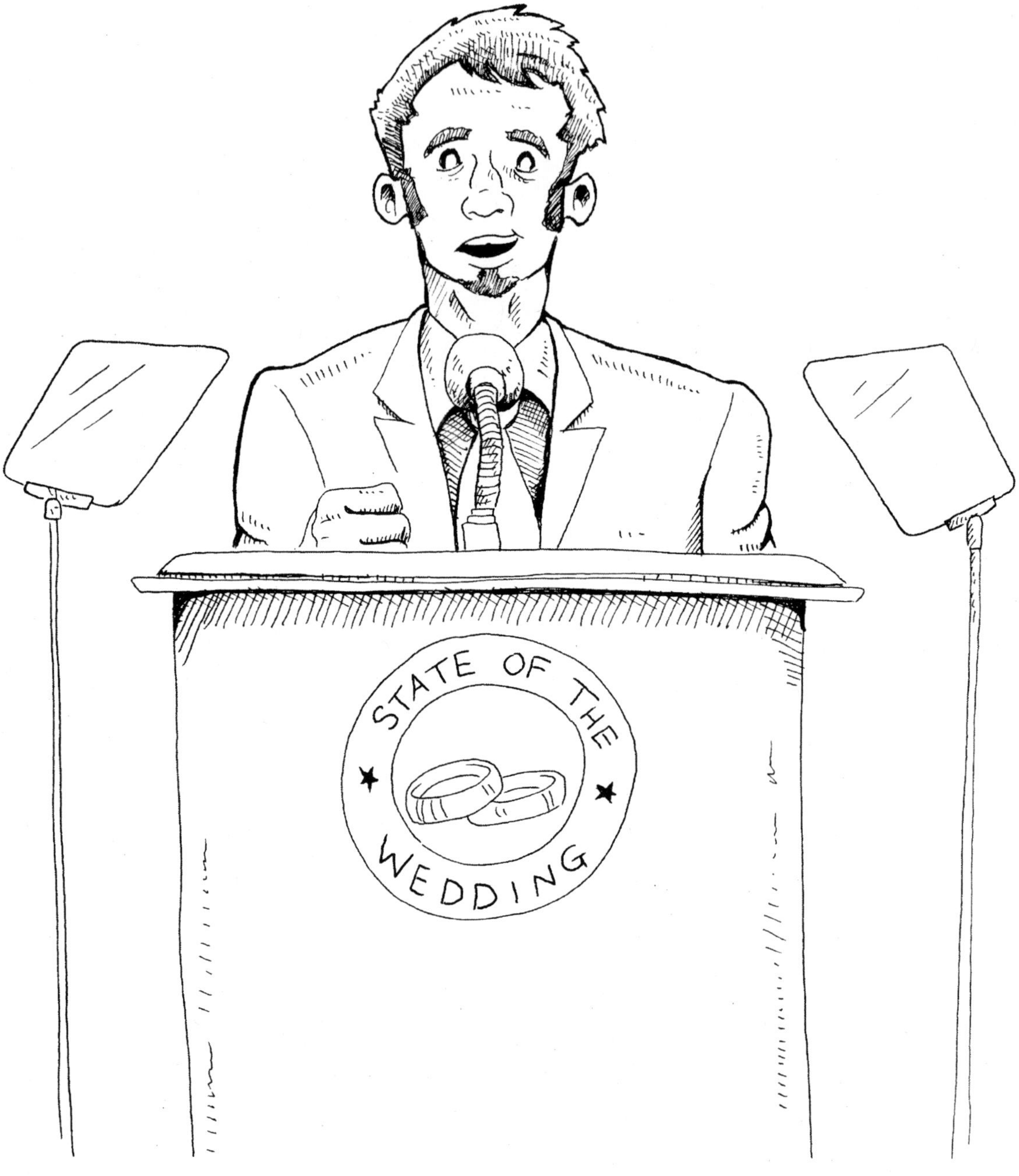
STATE OF THE
WEDDING

11

DON'T allow toasts that turn into novels

Mention to your "toasters" beforehand to keep it to a reasonable length. Our record length at a wedding was 22:32. Yes, that's twenty-two minutes and thirty-two seconds—the length of a sit-com without commercials. And we have it on film, which is even worse. Do you think anyone is ever gonna watch that portion of the wedding video? Hell no. Keep it short and sweet, no longer than three minutes unless it's going to be really good and funny.

12

DON'T get married on a holiday weekend

Wouldn't it be great to have your wedding over a three-day weekend? Maybe for you, but is that really what your wedding day is about—you? But seriously, it might be convenient for you and your traveled family on such weekends, but not for the bulk of your guests. People we talk to cherish Memorial Day, Labor Day, and Fourth of July weekends, but what they are looking forward to is taking a long weekend and spending time with their families, not having to stick around town for your wedding. Let's face it, your family and friends do want to come to your wedding, but they would rather be on the lake soaking up rays during the only three extended weekends during the wedding season. We're sorry, but don't ruin these weekends, folks.

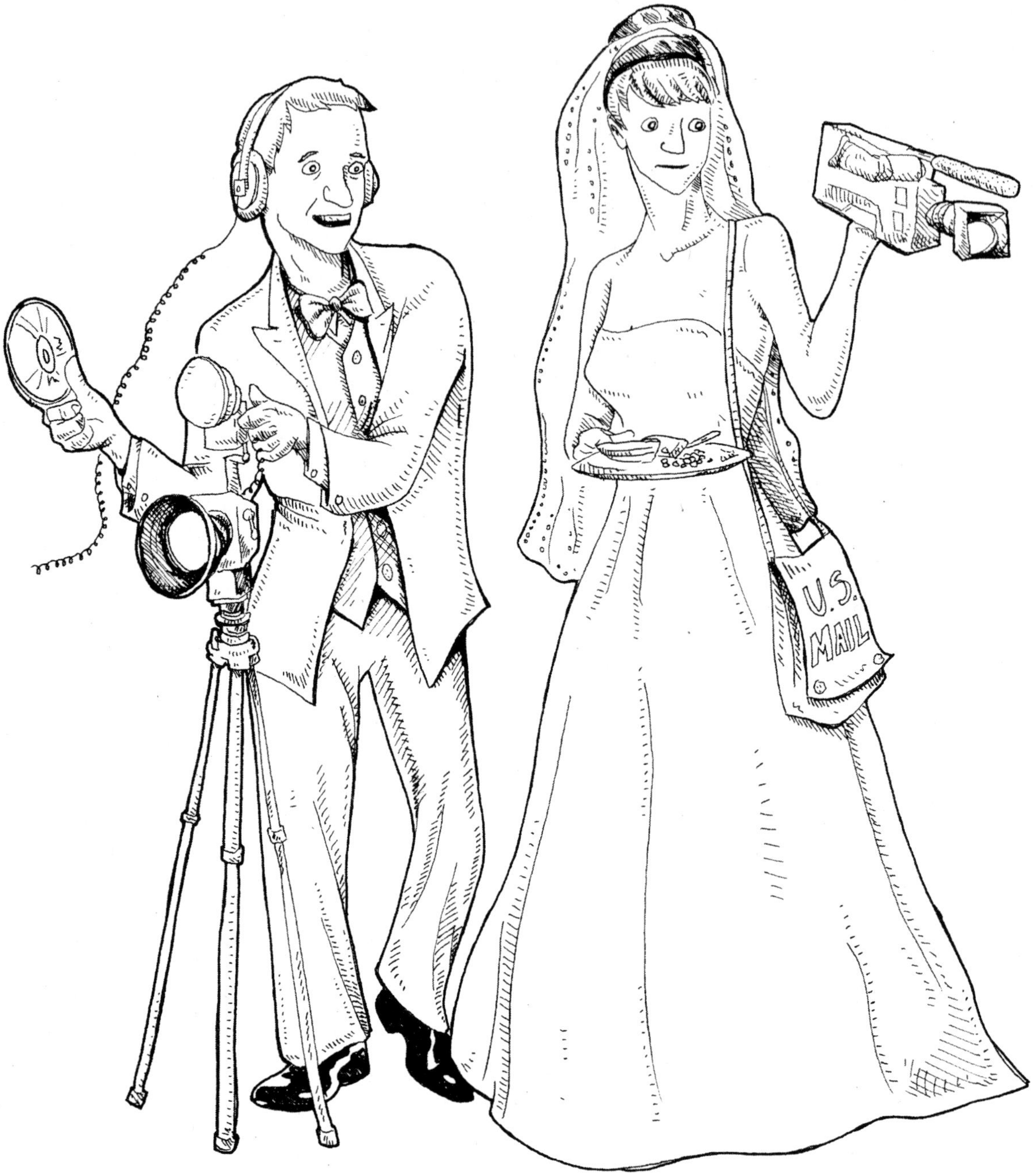
U.S.
MAIL

13

DON'T tell your vendors how to do their jobs

Do you tell your mailman how to deliver mail? Didn't think so. Think about it—you are not a DJ. You do not take photos for a living. And you do not think of yourself as a video professional. It is for these reasons that we say: "Do not tell your vendors how to perform their jobs." Please understand this is much different from telling vendors what you expect from them. Yes! Tell them what you expect, but just do not ever start barking orders about how to make these expectations come true.

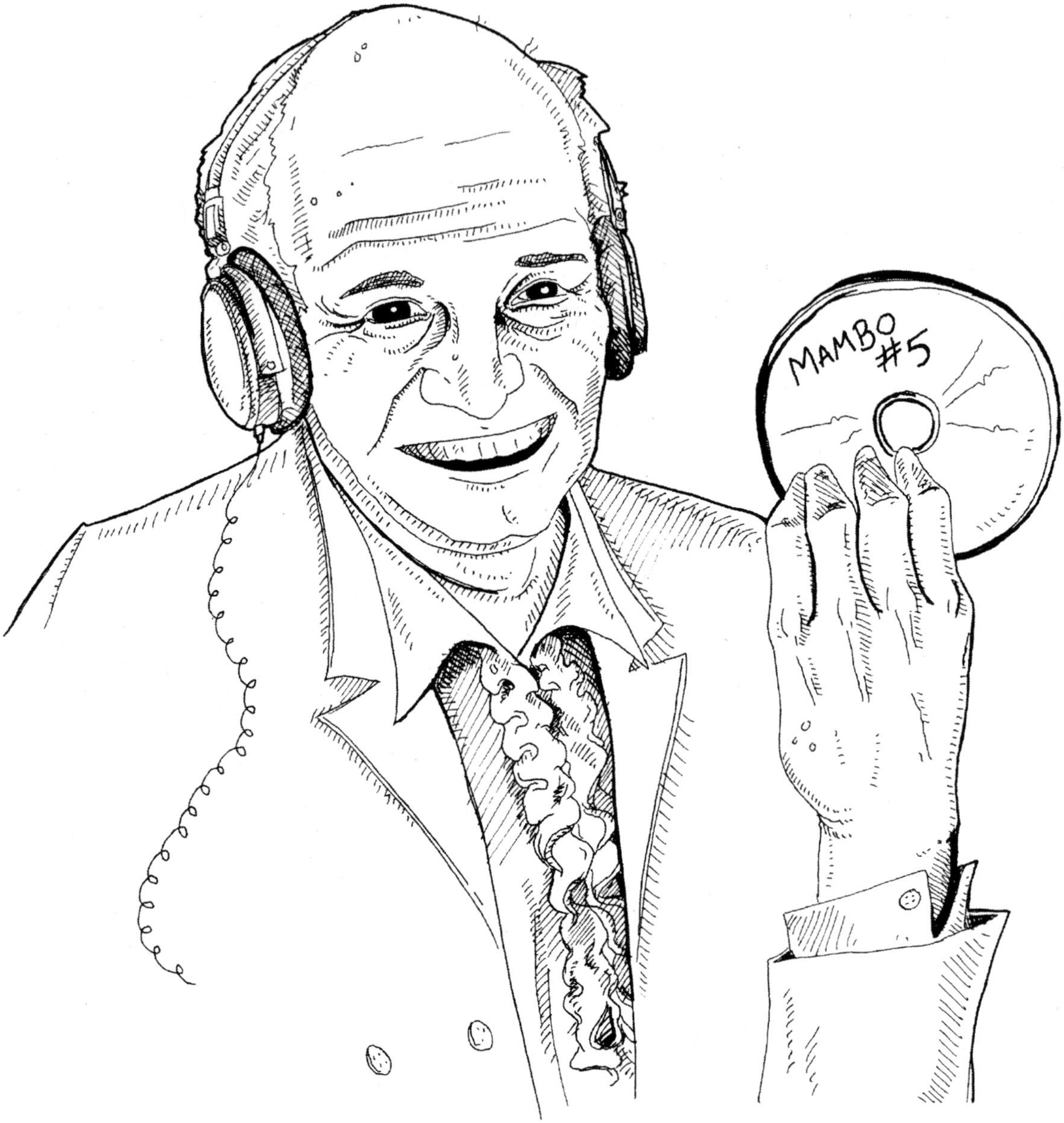
MAMBO #5

14

DON'T hire an old DJ

Funny reason, eh? Well, it is definitely a no-no. If you hire an old DJ, then you will end up having an old guy entertaining at your wedding—the key phrase here is "old guy." Old guys should be checking their blood pressure, not DJing weddings. Doing this usually equals a ton of "really great" tunes such as "Mambo #5" and "The Macarena." The problem: The old guy actually thinks these are really great tunes. Just don't get mad at us at 9:00 PM when you are asking yourself: "Where the hell did everyone go?"

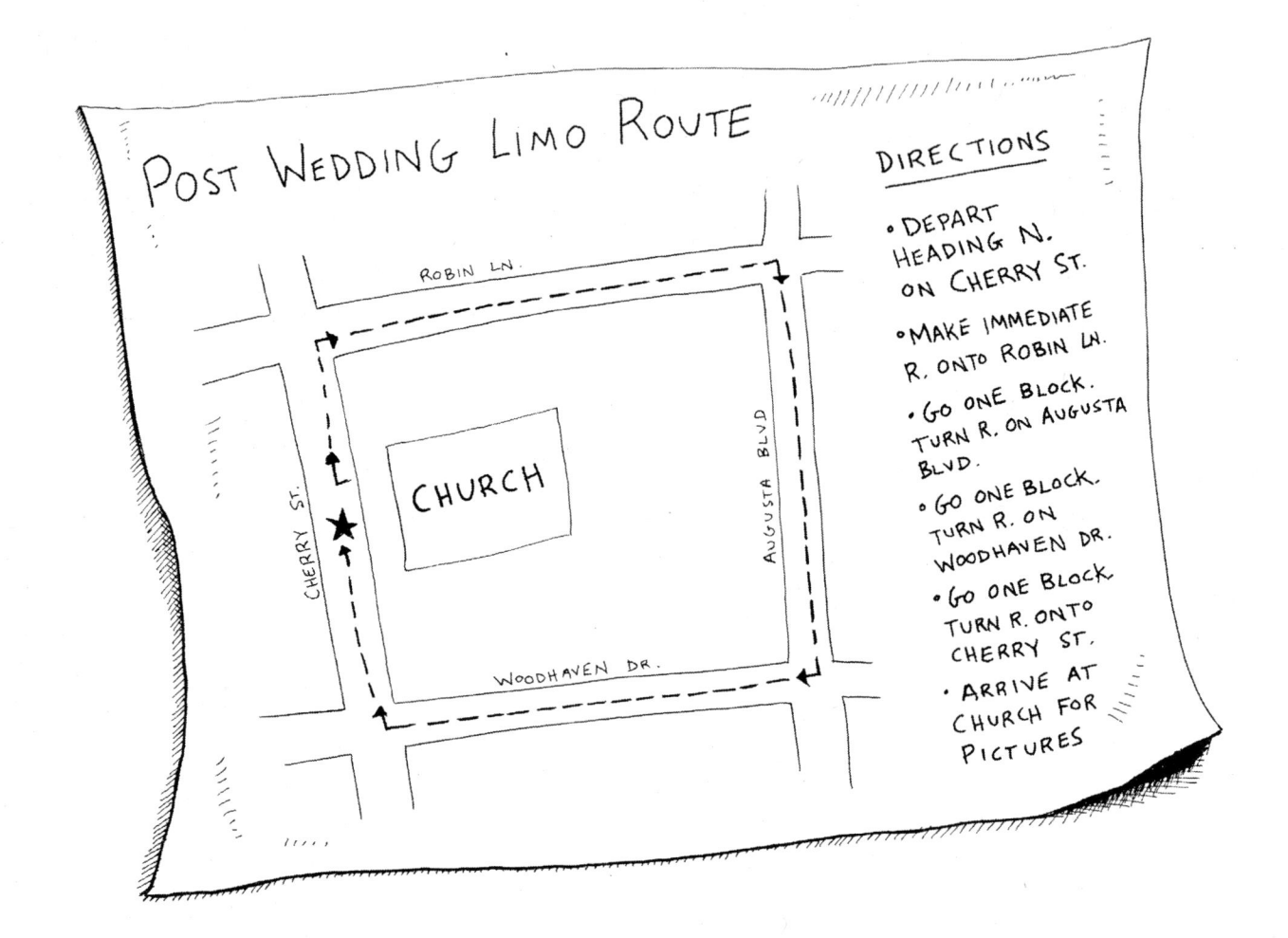

Post Wedding Limo Route

Directions

- Depart heading N. on Cherry St.
- Make immediate R. onto Robin Ln.
- Go one block. Turn R. on Augusta Blvd.
- Go one block. Turn R. on Woodhaven Dr.
- Go one block. Turn R. onto Cherry St.
- Arrive at Church for Pictures

15

DON'T wait until after the ceremony to take family pictures

Have you ever waited around outside for a few minutes after the bride and groom leave from the church in their limo? If you have, then you know they usually just come right back and go into the church to take an endless array of photos. Now—doesn't all of that "postwedding limo sendoff" hoopla all of a sudden just seem silly and fake? Take your pictures before the wedding, get into the limo, and actually leave. Go have fun and enjoy yourself, and maybe you will be able to show up for your own cocktail hour. After all, everyone is there to see you.

36

16

DON'T have your reception in a "unique" place

The word "unique" in this case means a place that you think is totally cool and different, such as your favorite Mexican restaurant or your rich Uncle Albert's backyard. But these types of locations actually turn out to be more of a pain when it comes to all the important details and logistics of your evening. For instance, where is the dance floor going to be at your favorite restaurant? Does Uncle Albert have enough restrooms for 200 people? There are many issues like these that will cause problems.

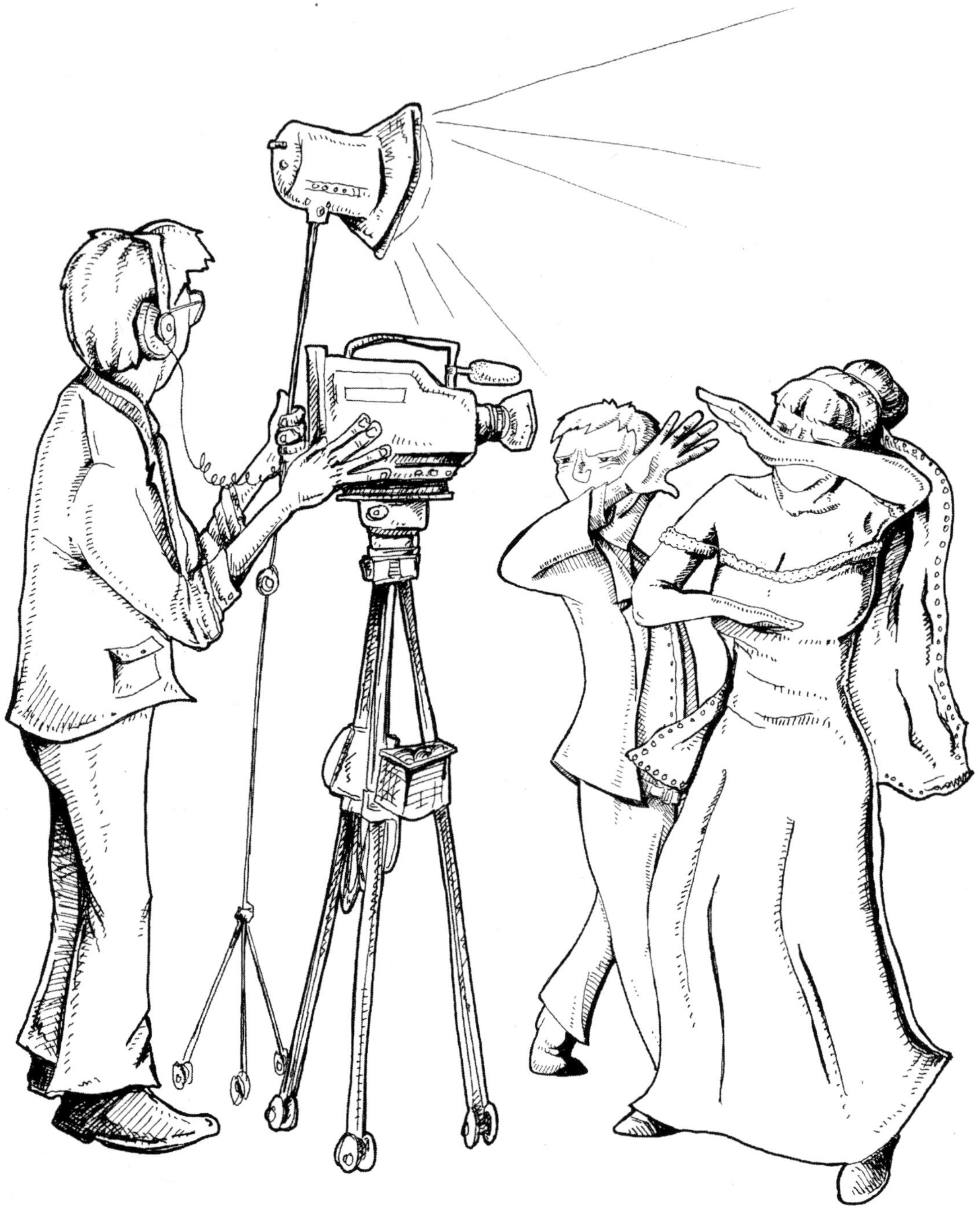

17

DON'T have your videographer document everything

Unless you have ever dreamed of being on MTV's Real World, then tell your videographer to back off. Yeah, he needs to get everything important on film and make it look nice, but there is no reason for a video camera on a tripod with rolling wheels and a light as bright as the sun skating around the dance floor while you are doing the "Casper Slide." Some memories just were not meant to be captured on film.

The Life of a $75 Floral Arrangement

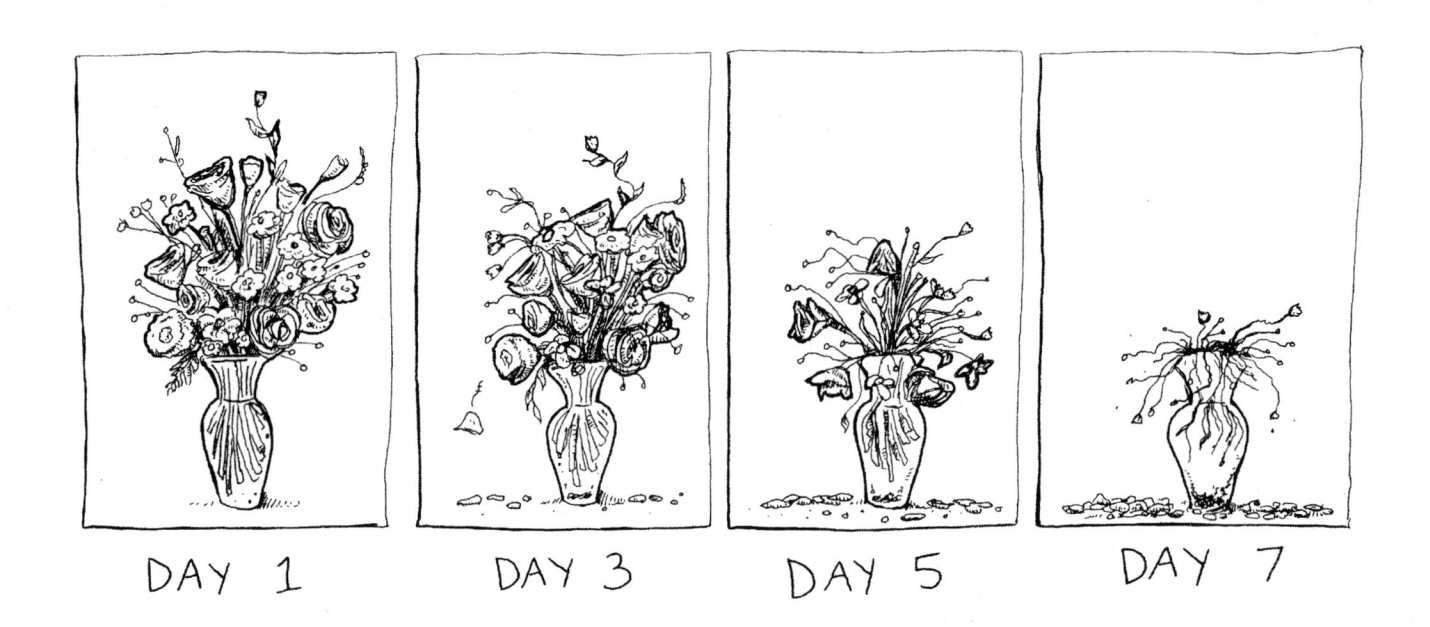

| DAY 1 | DAY 3 | DAY 5 | DAY 7 |

18

DON'T spend a fortune on flowers

OK ladies, we know we are guys, and guys don't generally have a taste for flowers, but please hear us out. We have two main points regarding flowers. First, flowers are expensive, and second, flowers die quickly. A few subtle flowers are very nice, but the wedding is already so expensive that we do not feel it is necessary to spend another $1,000+ on a bunch of pretty objects that will die before the end of your honeymoon.

NOT FANCY   STILL NOT FANCY

19

DON'T add shaved almonds to the green beans

Shaved almonds, toasted almonds, or any other nut do not make green beans fancy. In fact, we do not think there is any way to make green beans fancy. Instead of adding a shaved nut to increase value, try selecting a new vegetable first. We suggest asparagus, baby zucchini, or a nice glazed carrot.

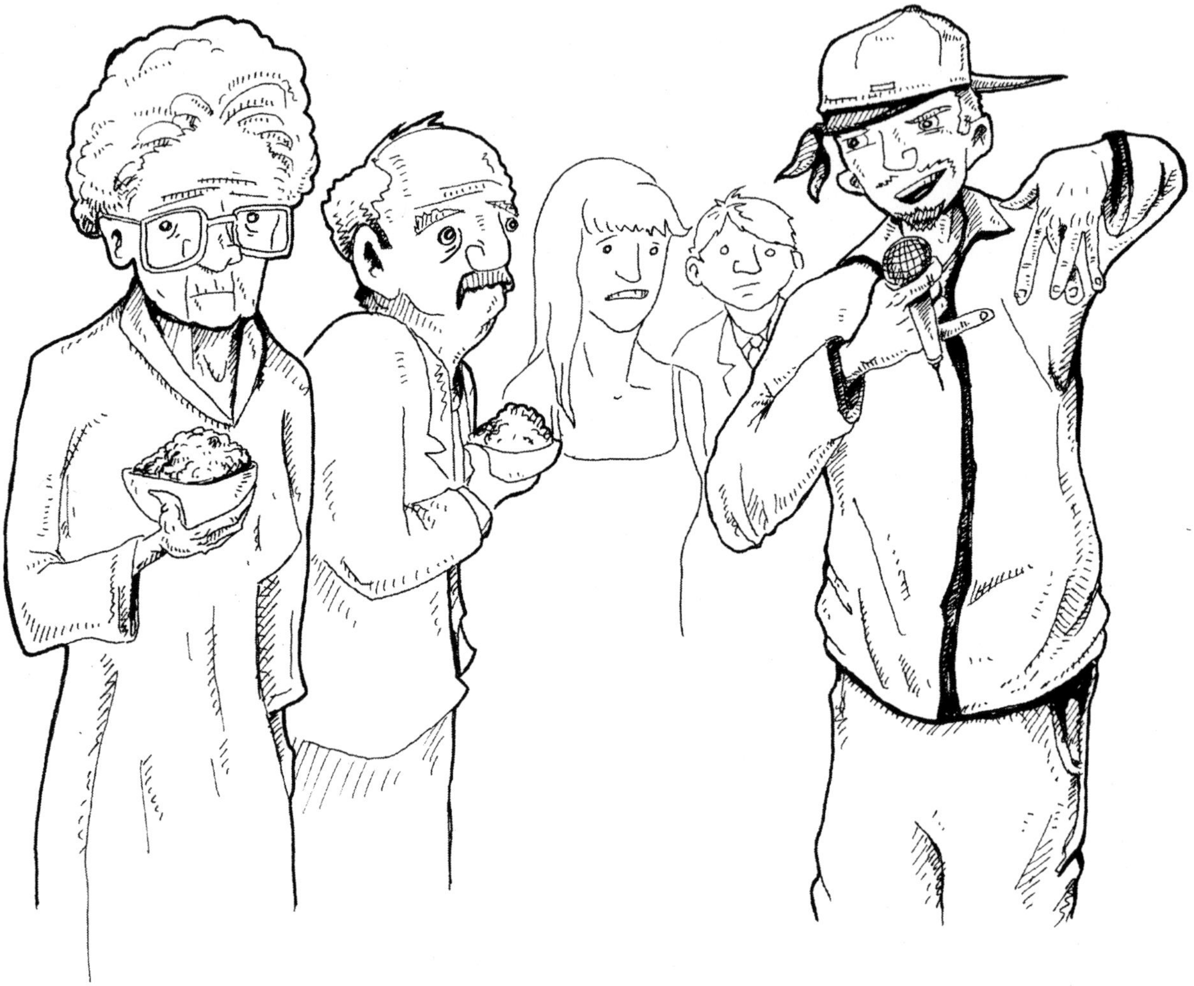

20

DON'T plan everything around only what you like

But, it's your wedding, right? Yes, your wedding is mostly about you and your future spouse, but what about the 250 guests that will be traveling long distances to spend the day with you? You must think of your guests as well in order to have a successful wedding. This means that your love for babaghanoush and gangster rap music might need to be put on hold for the night.

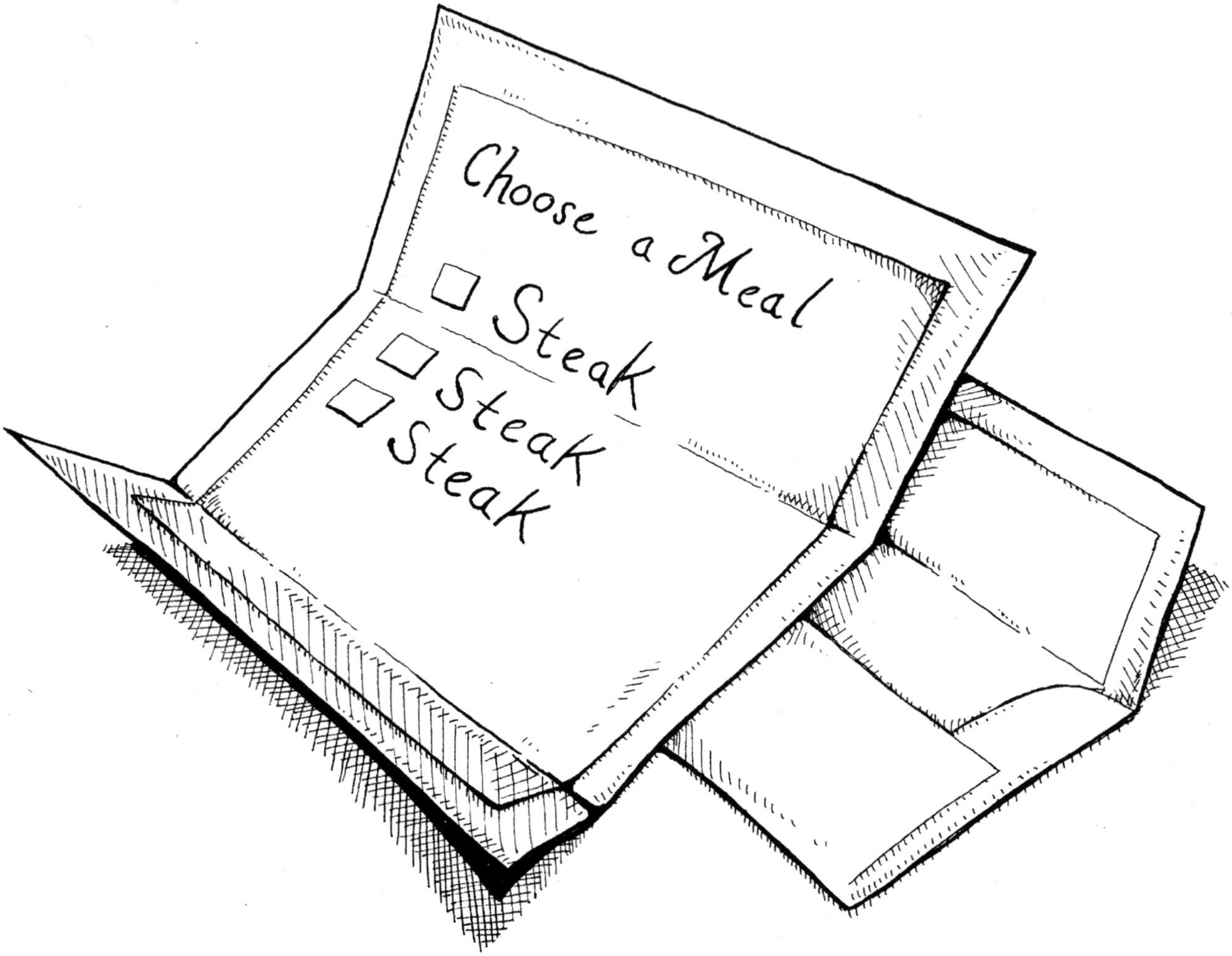
Choose a Meal
Steak
Steak
Steak

21

DON'T offer just one meal selection

I want steak! I want tofu! I want peanut butter and marshmallows! Yes, these are your friends, folks. You certainly will never be able to make everyone happy—that is for sure. But you can do your best to offer something that everyone will be able to enjoy. Offering a selection of meals is very important. It will take some more effort in the invitation and organization process, but it is well worth it. Your banquet coordinator and caterer will hate you for it because it makes more work for themselves and the kitchen. But who cares—it's your wedding, remember? Try a choice between a filet with a red wine sauce, roasted red potatoes, asparagus, and pearl onions or a halibut dish with a citrus butter sauce, creamy polenta, and sautéed zucchini, carrots, and shallots or a roasted garlic and wild mushroom risotto topped with fresh parsley and chives as a vegetarian option.

48

22

DON'T have a summer wedding without A/C

Sounds obvious, right? Well, we wish it was, but it seems to happen all the time. No A/C will result in a miserable experience for everyone, but especially for the guys. Women can wear light open-air dresses while men are forced to dress up with no air circulation to look like penguins. It's simple. If men have to dress like penguins, then the temperature better be suitable for a penguin.

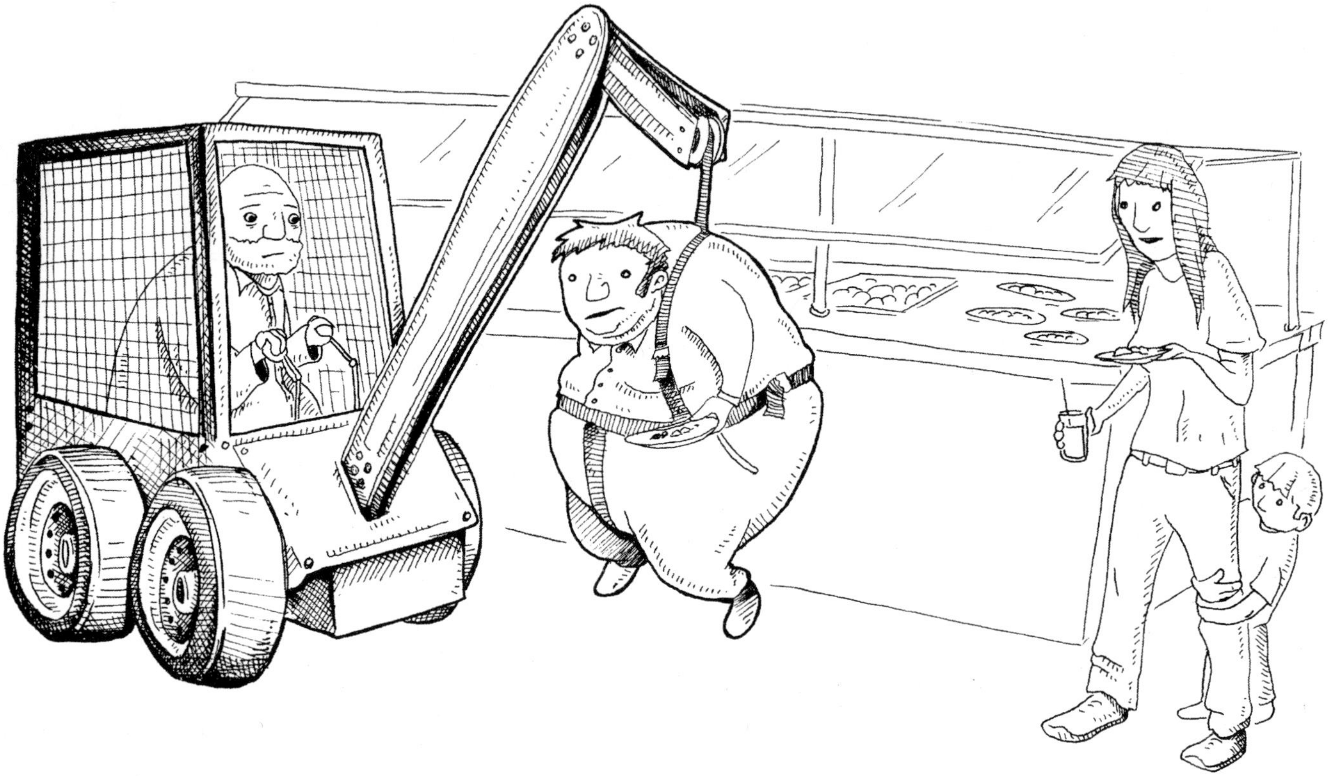

23

DON'T choose a reception hall with different floors

Reception halls with multiple levels might seem cool and different, but they really just cause problems. For instance, moving a group of 175 guests up or down stairs is like moving a 300-pound man from the dinner line during ½ price night at Old Country Buffet—it just ain't gonna be easy.

24

DON'T place your bar away from the dance floor

Women typically want to dance. Men typically want to stand around the bar and drink. Now, try and get those guys to a dance floor that is all the way across the room—that is just too far for most guys to venture away from the bar. Put your dance floor close to the bar and more people will flock to it.

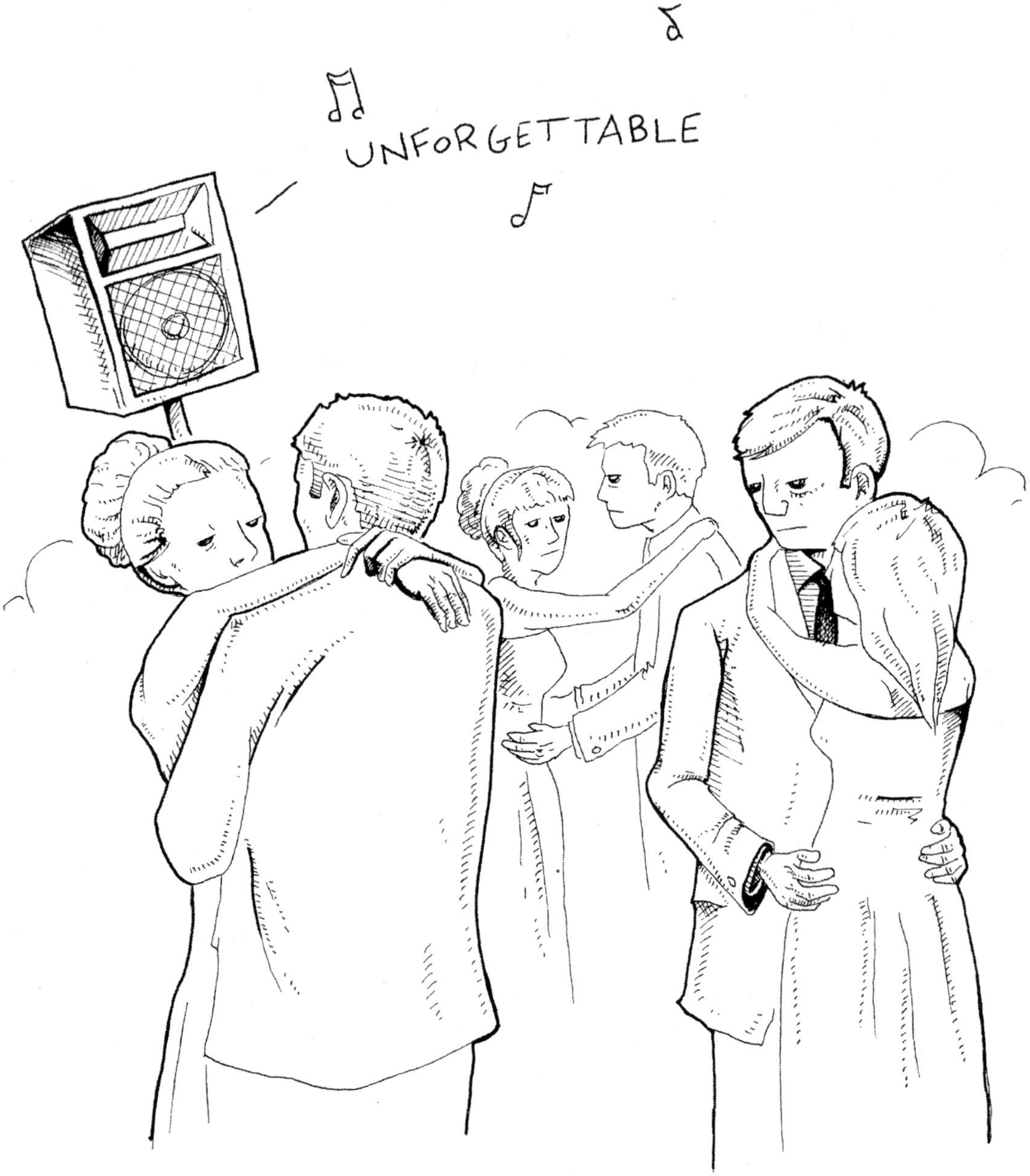
UNFORGETTABLE

∞ 25 ∞

DON'T have a wedding party dance

It's time to face the music, folks. Nobody likes the wedding party dance...especially the wedding party.

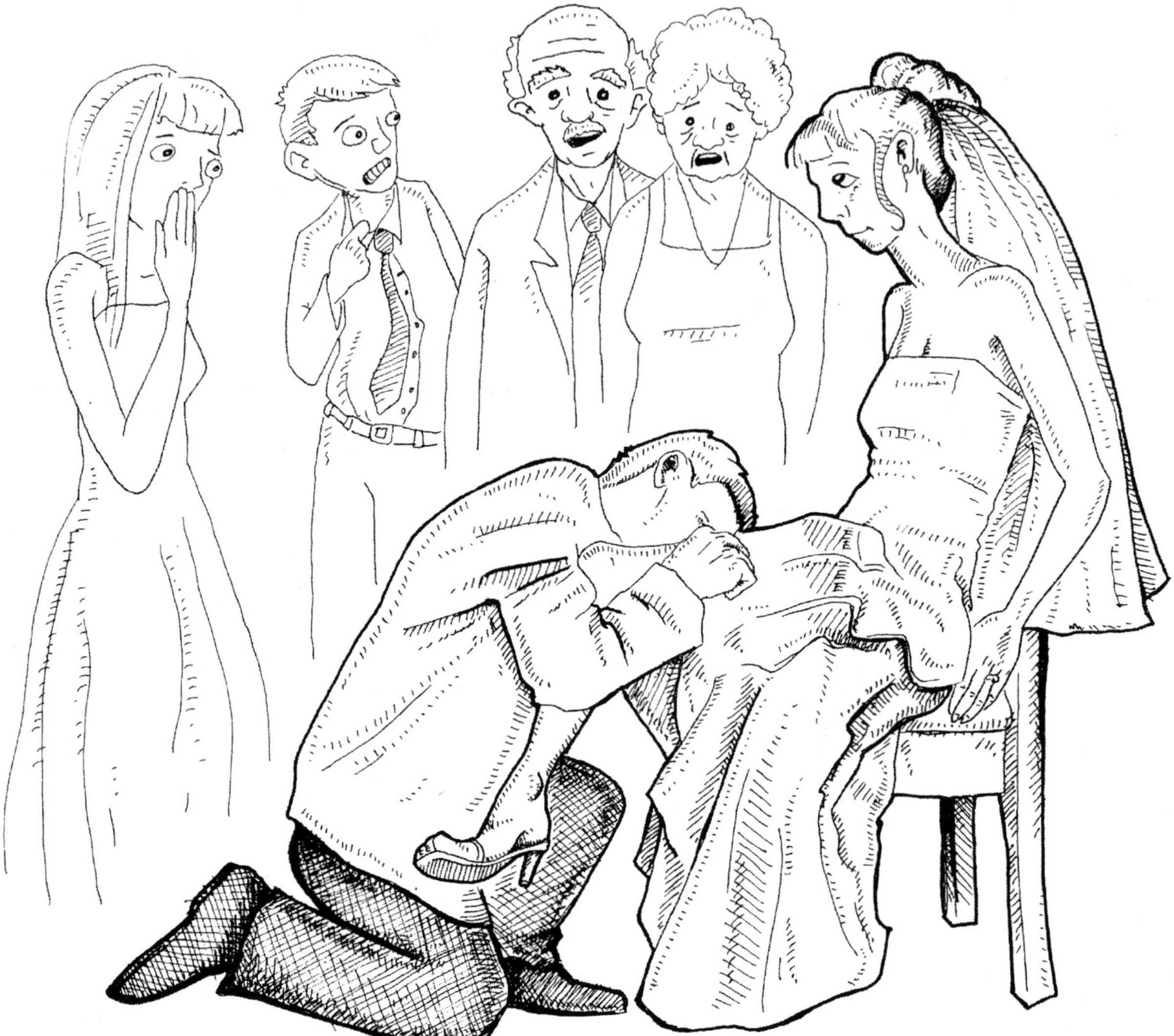

26

DON'T do the bouquet and garter toss

We know, we know—its tradition, right? But whoever said you had to follow in everyone's footsteps? The bouquet toss is one thing, but the garter toss is a bit disturbing. Believe me, every single person standing around that dance floor has an uncomfortable feeling inside as they watch the groom go "down under" and strip off the bride's garter. What most people actually end up watching is the bride's parents and grandparents, thinking "man, this must be weird for them." It's time to come up with a new tradition.

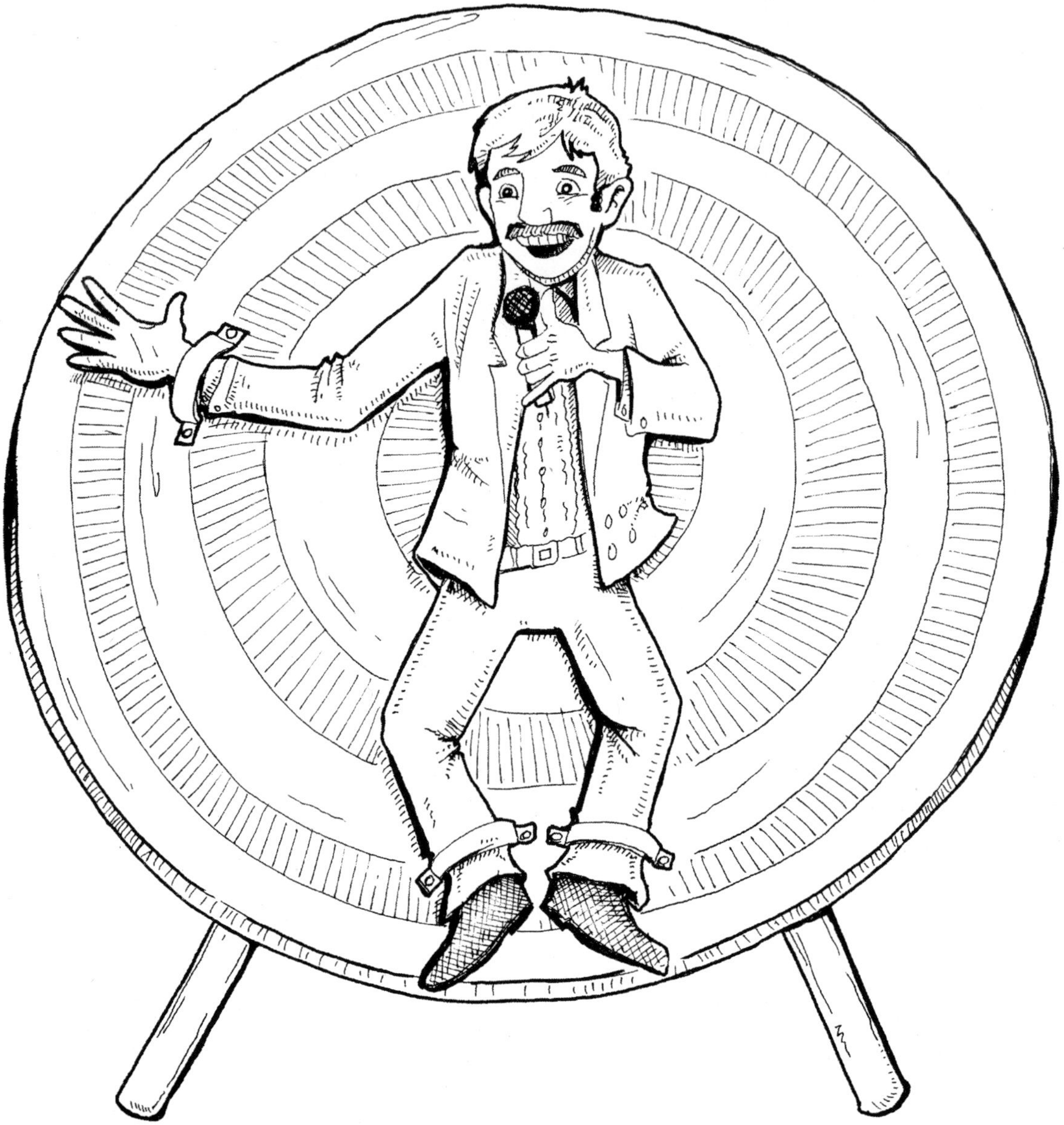

27

DON'T make your guests form a big circle on the dance floor

Yes, you know what we are talking about—the dreaded Hokey Pokey and Chicken Dance. And we do not use the word "dreaded" here lightly. These typical wedding participation dances often make guests shiver in anguish when they hear the DJ say: "OK let's get everyone out on the dance floor in a big circle." The only circle your guests will want at that point is a big red one on the DJ's forehead.

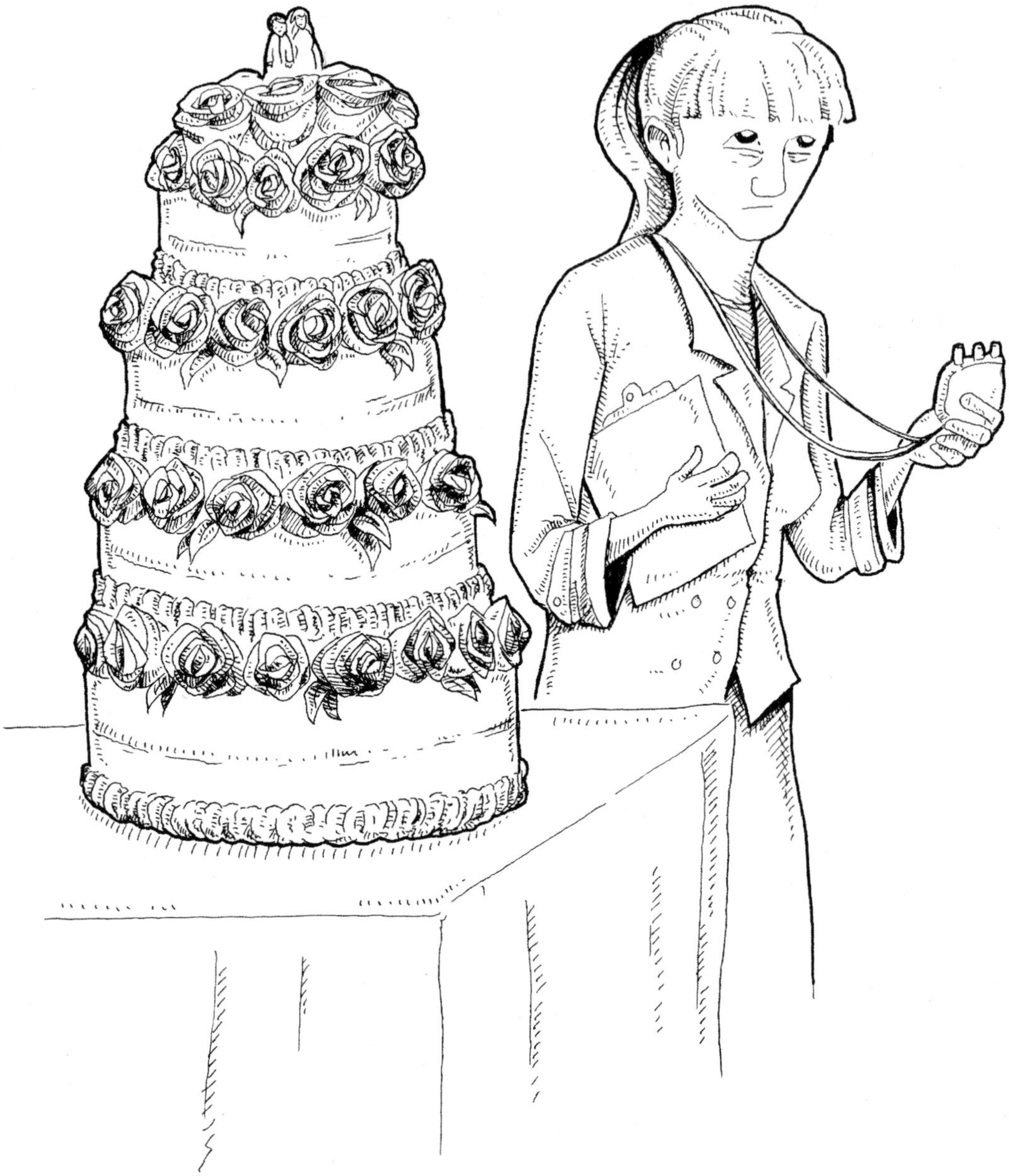

28

DON'T let your caterer tell you when to cut the cake

Is the wedding cake important to you? Yes? Really, yes? Well, if it is so important, then let it sit out there for awhile so you can enjoy looking at it. We guarantee that the caterer will want you to cut it right after your arrival, but you are the one that spent $1,000 on a bunch of flour and sugar, and so you should be the one to choose when to destroy it. Again, folks, this is to make it easier for the caterer so they have more time to cut the pieces. Of course, you need to allow time for cutting, but it does not take two hours to cut 150 pieces of cake.

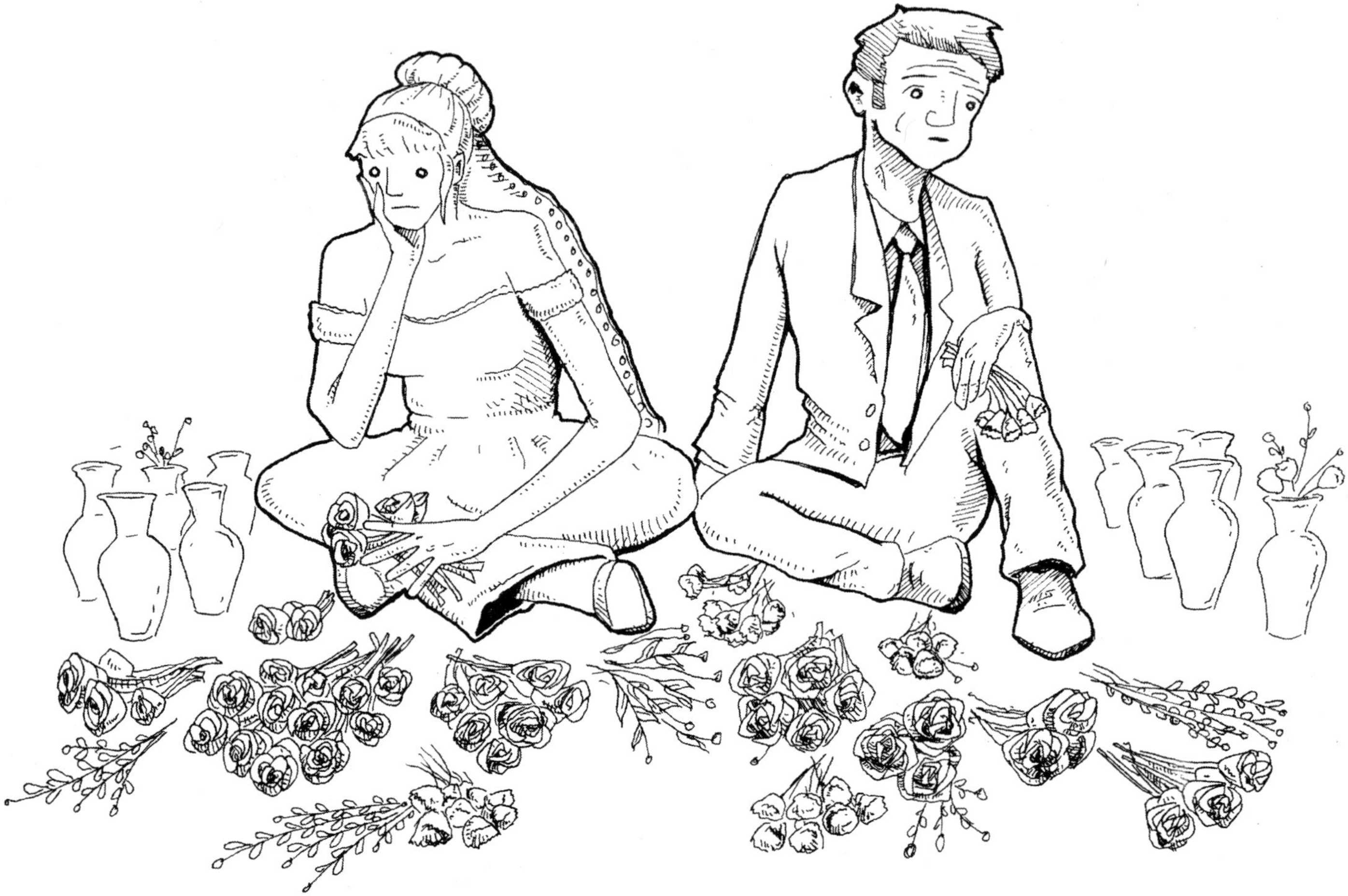

29

DON'T make the flowers yourself

Listen, you have enough to do to plan and get ready for the big day. Do not attempt to do something that you are not qualified to do. Making your own flowers takes an immense amount of time you don't have, as well as a skill that you haven't acquired. Good friends of ours attempted to do this, and it was a disaster. They realized there was not enough time and had to pay a florist rush charges to complete their attempt. If you are making the flowers yourself because you want to save money, then please review our reason #18 again for an important floral refresher.

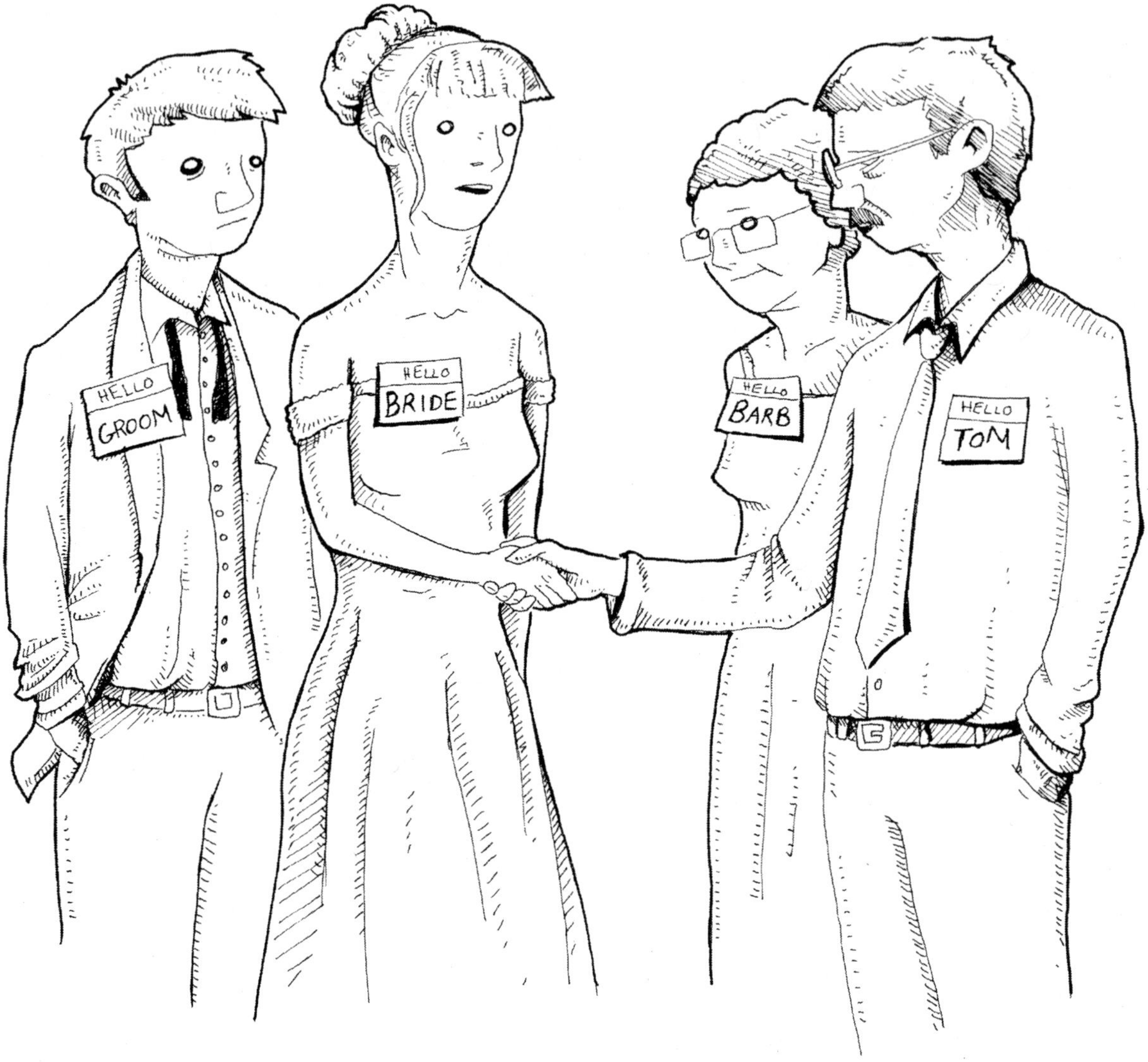
HELLO
GROOM
HELLO
BRIDE
HELLO
BARB
HELLO
TOM

30

DON'T forget to invite your friends

Your parents might be chipping in a chunk of cash for your wedding gala, but what is the point in the investment if you do not invite all the important people in your life? If you think your parents are paying because they indirectly want to get all their friends and business contacts together while limiting the number of people you can invite, then you should probably discuss this immediately. While they may be footing the bill, it is still your wedding. You need to make sure that you have the final say on who can and cannot attend. Otherwise, might we suggest name badges so you can better get to know all of the strangers you will be meeting at your wedding?

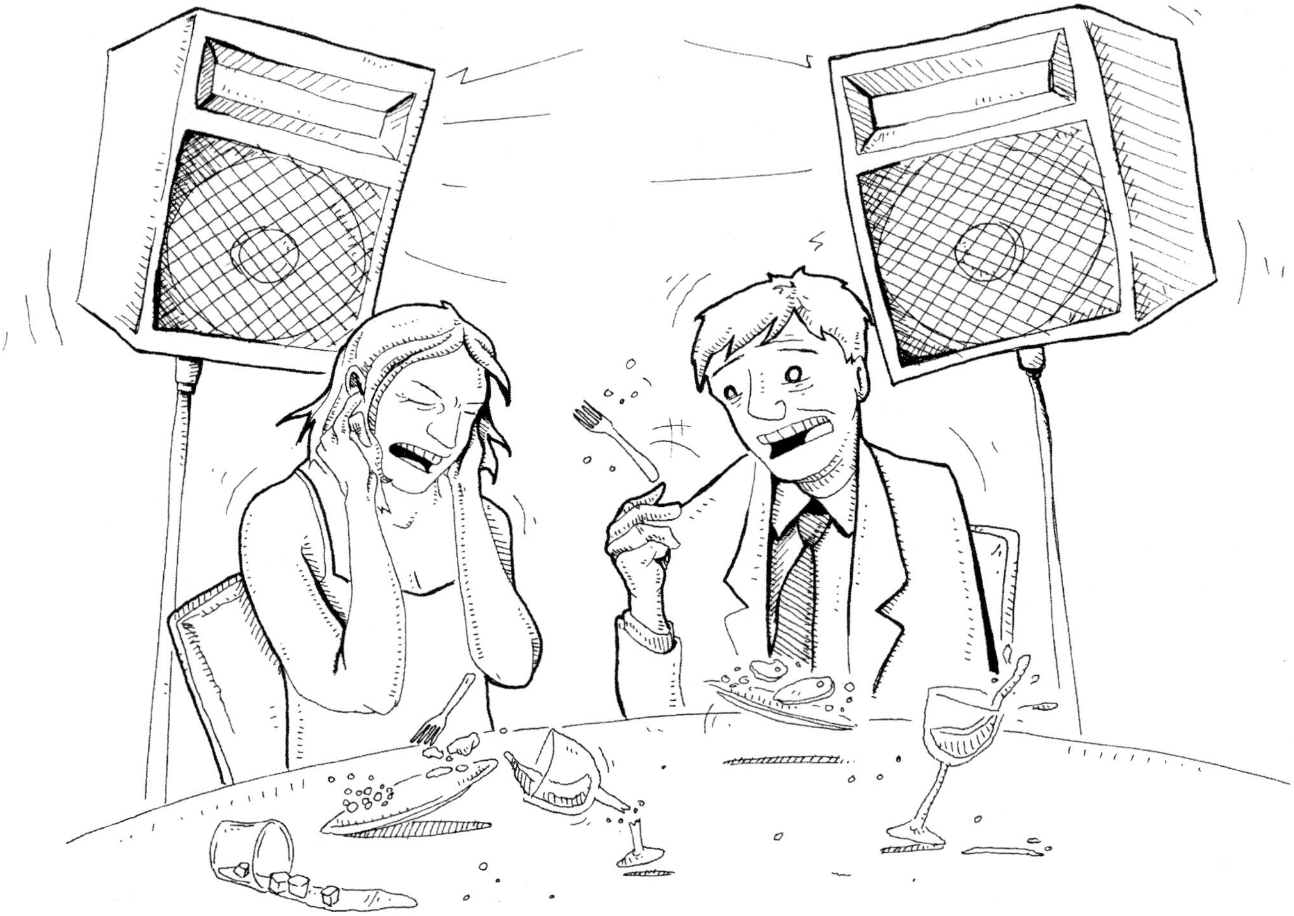

31

DON'T put tables in between the dance floor and the DJ

Unless you have a group of deaf people attending your wedding, you should never put tables between the dance floor and DJ. The DJ has to project music to the dance floor through large speakers. Having tables in the path of that music is a bad idea. All night long the people in the path will be asking for the music to be lowered, while the people dancing will be asking for it to be raised. And let us tell you—DJs just love this.

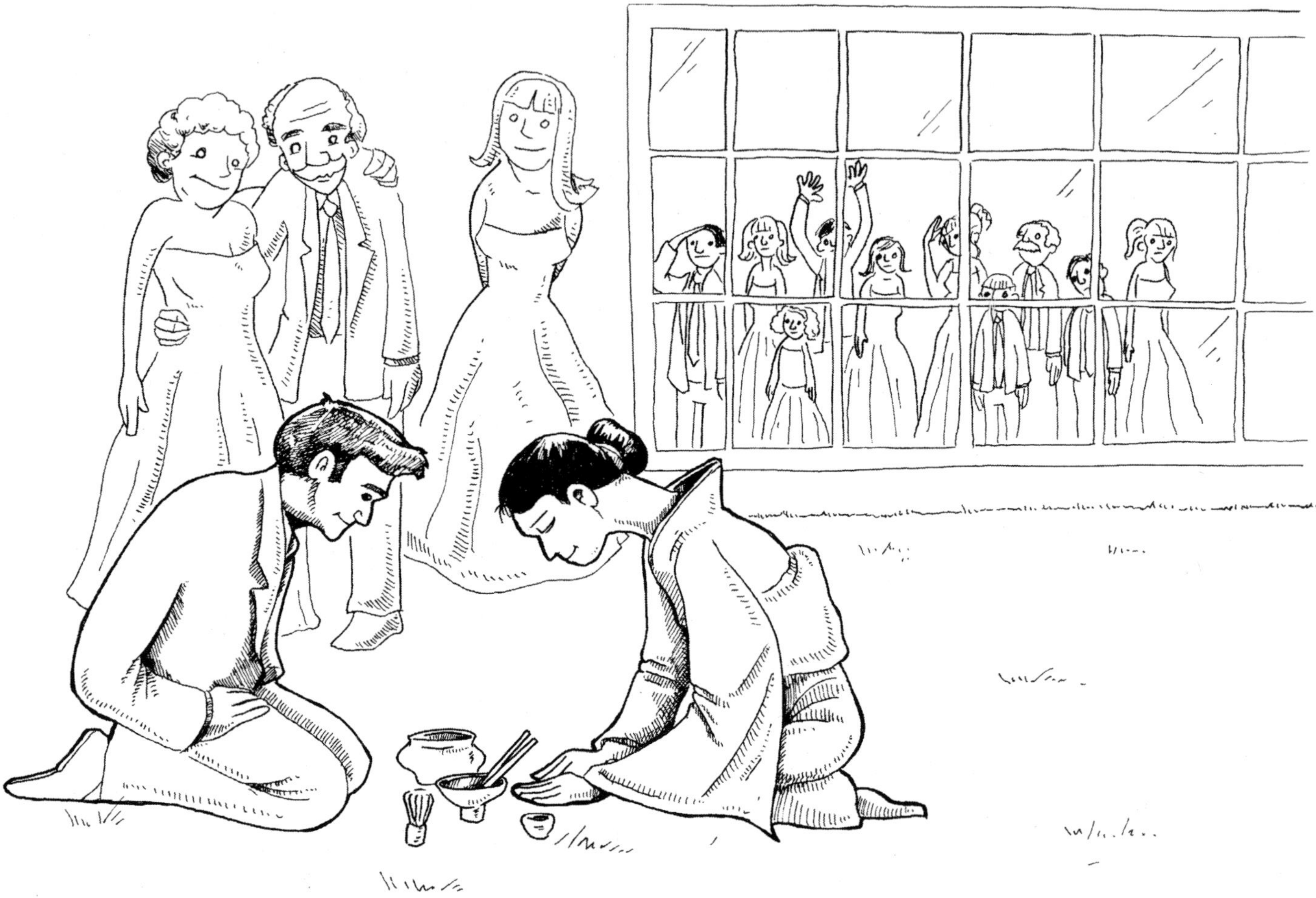

32

DON'T have a special ceremony during your reception

You may want to have a special tea ceremony or other private religious ceremony at your wedding, but doing this during your reception is about as good an idea as eating a second enchilada at the prewedding lunch. If you and your close family and friends disappear for an extended period of time, people will start to leave. Why? Well, because they think you left. Not only is it rude to invite only specific people to a private ceremony, but it is also a very huge waste of precious and very expensive reception time. Remember, people came to see and hang out with you.

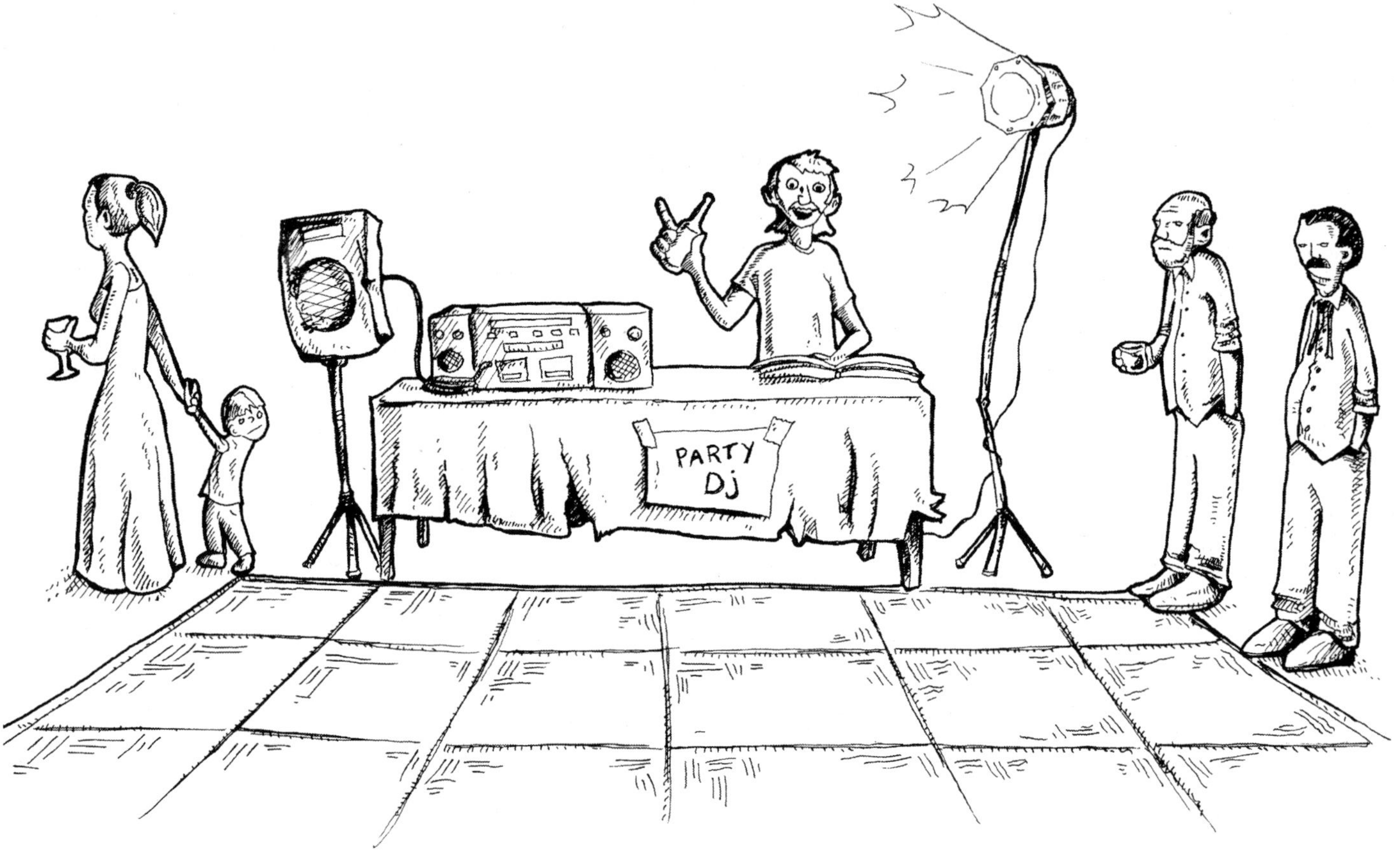
PARTY
Dj

33

DON'T hire a random DJ

Most brides wouldn't dare hire a wedding cake baker without meeting her first and tasting her samples. And the wedding cake is not all that important in the grand scheme of things (sorry, girls, it's true). The bottom line—your DJ is going to make or break your wedding. He creates the atmosphere for a party—no atmosphere equals no party. Research, ask friends, read reviews, and find a great DJ – they are out there. Meet your specific DJ in person, and go to see your DJ at an event before signing a contract. And make sure the specific DJ that you meet with is named in the contract. This will be worth the effort—believe us.

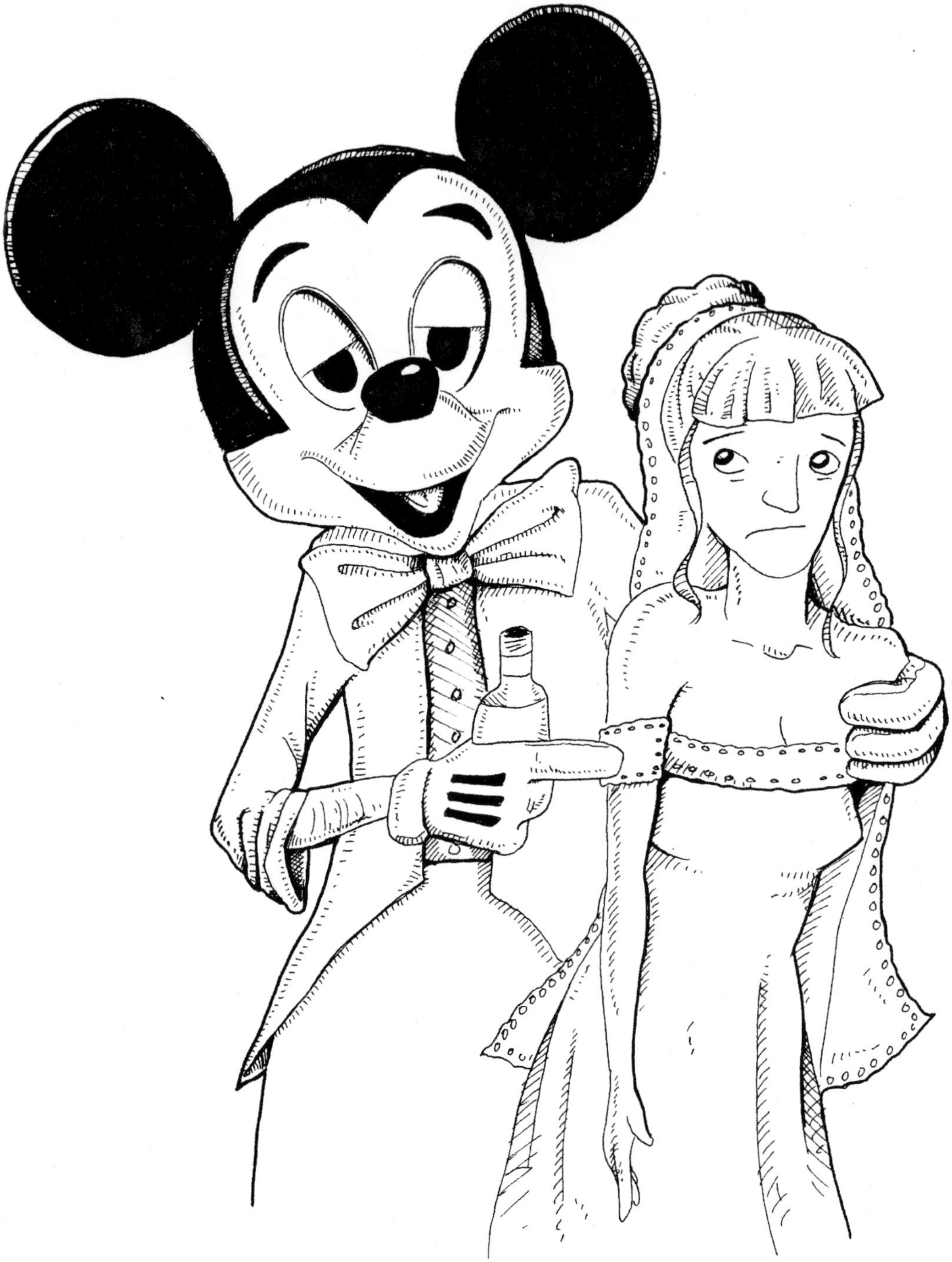

34

DON'T have a Disney-themed wedding

Please, just take our word here. We have seen it, and it was awful. Nobody wants to dance to "Hakuna Matata"—ever. What an awful idea!

74

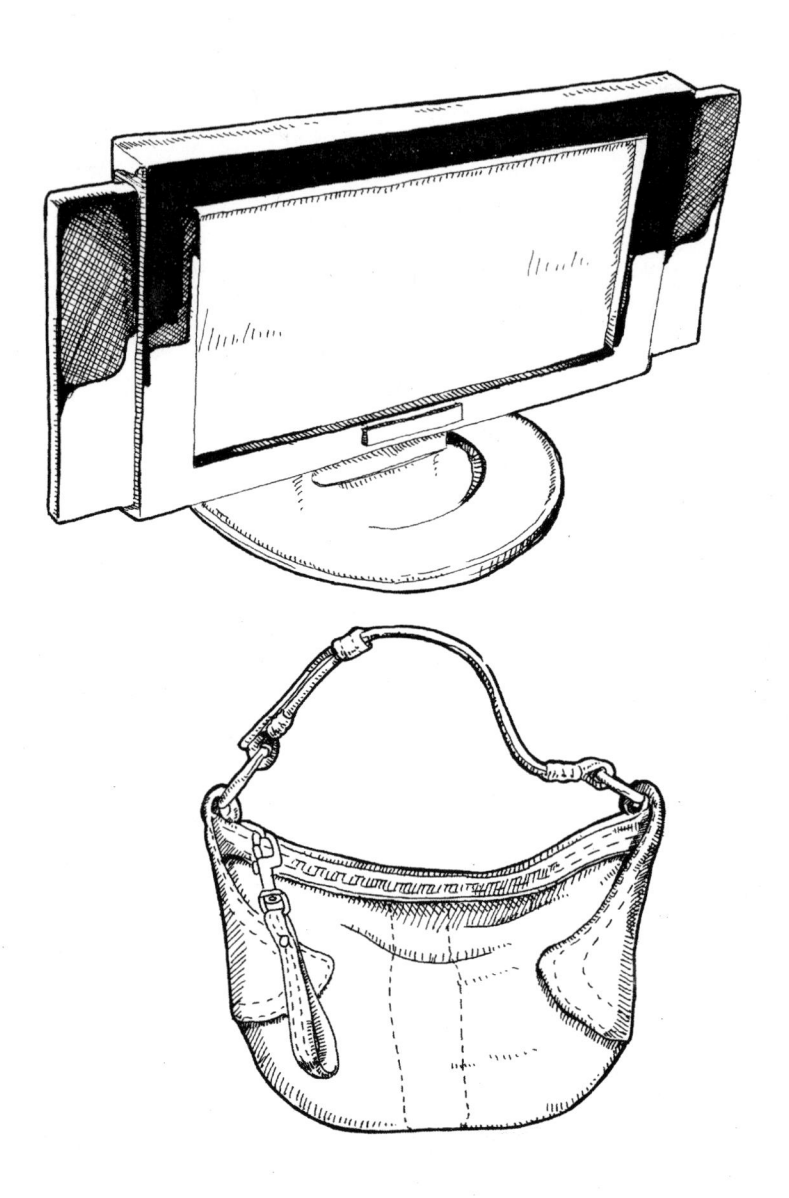

35

DON'T spend $10 for a white chair cover

Let me break this extreme waste of money down for you. At $10 a chair, you are paying $1,500 for 150 guests, $2,000 for 200 guests, and a whopping $3,000 if you have 300 guests. Can you believe it? We can't. This is the ultimate frivolous wedding expense of all time. We are sure that chairs with cute little white covers will look nice, but so would a brand new 65" HD flat panel in the living room of your new home. Or, for the ladies, a Coach handbag including all accessories. We'd get the TV.

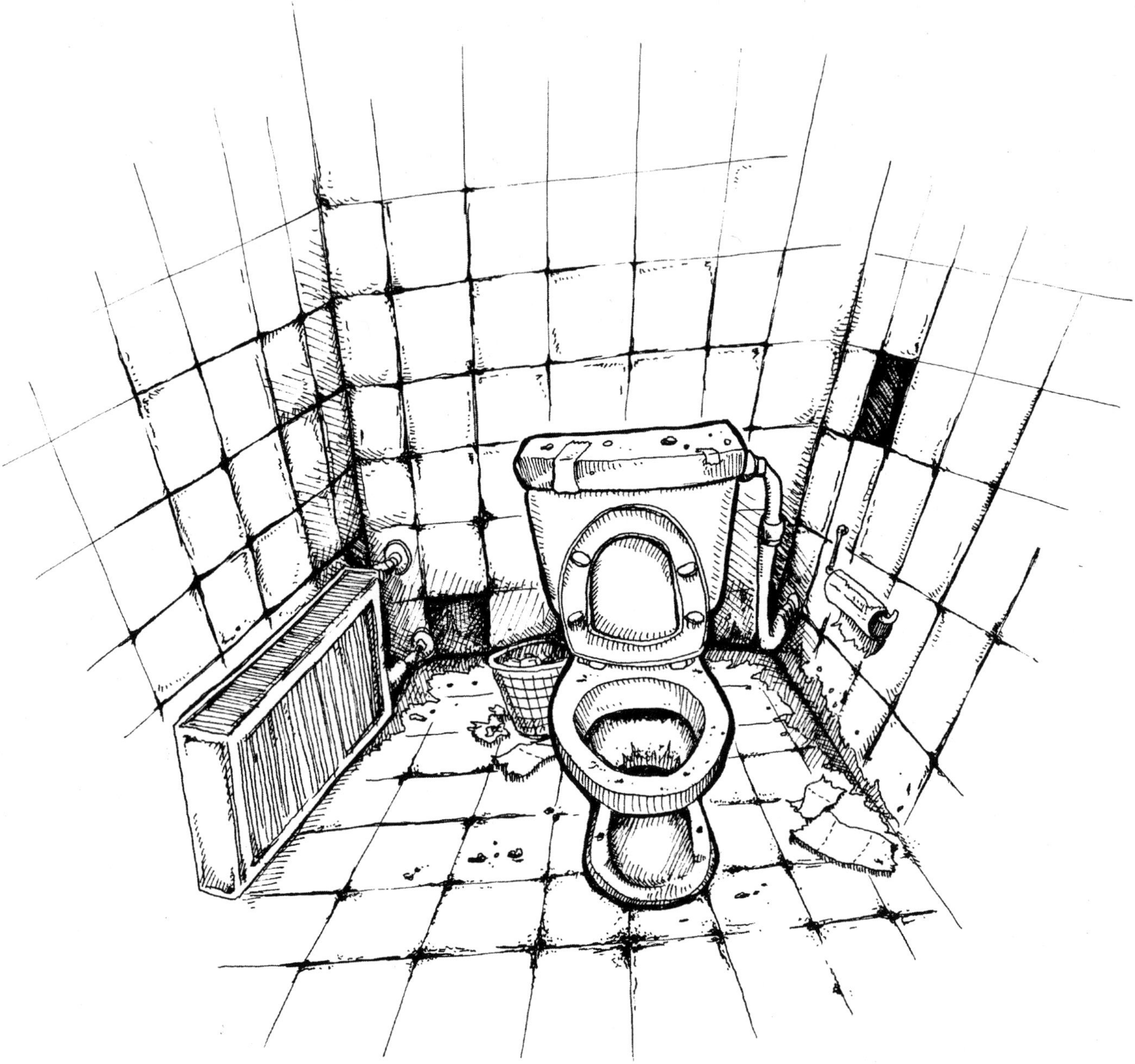

36

DON'T forget to check out the facilities at the reception hall

Remember, people will have to go to the bathroom at your wedding, especially if you go with the flaming saganaki for an appetizer. Make sure they have a nice, clean place to sit. Nobody likes to hover if they don't have to.

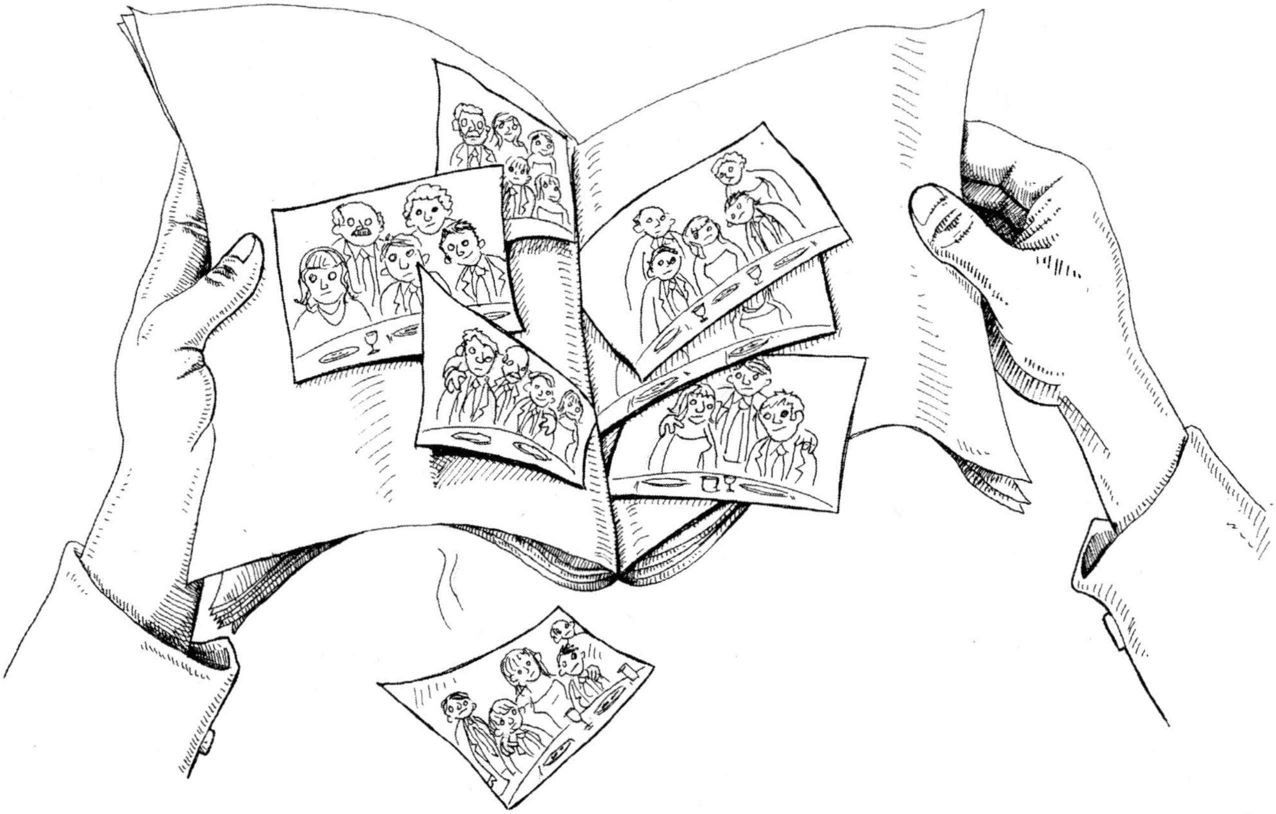

37

DON'T subject your guests to group table photos

If your wedding album was a magazine, then the group table photos would be like those annoying subscription cards that fall out with the turn of every page. These photos serve no purpose other than to remind you that everyone did in fact eat the dinner you spent half of your life savings on. It is very annoying for your guests to have to get up during the meal and uncomfortably crowd on one end of the table to pose for a photo that everyone knows no one is going to buy.

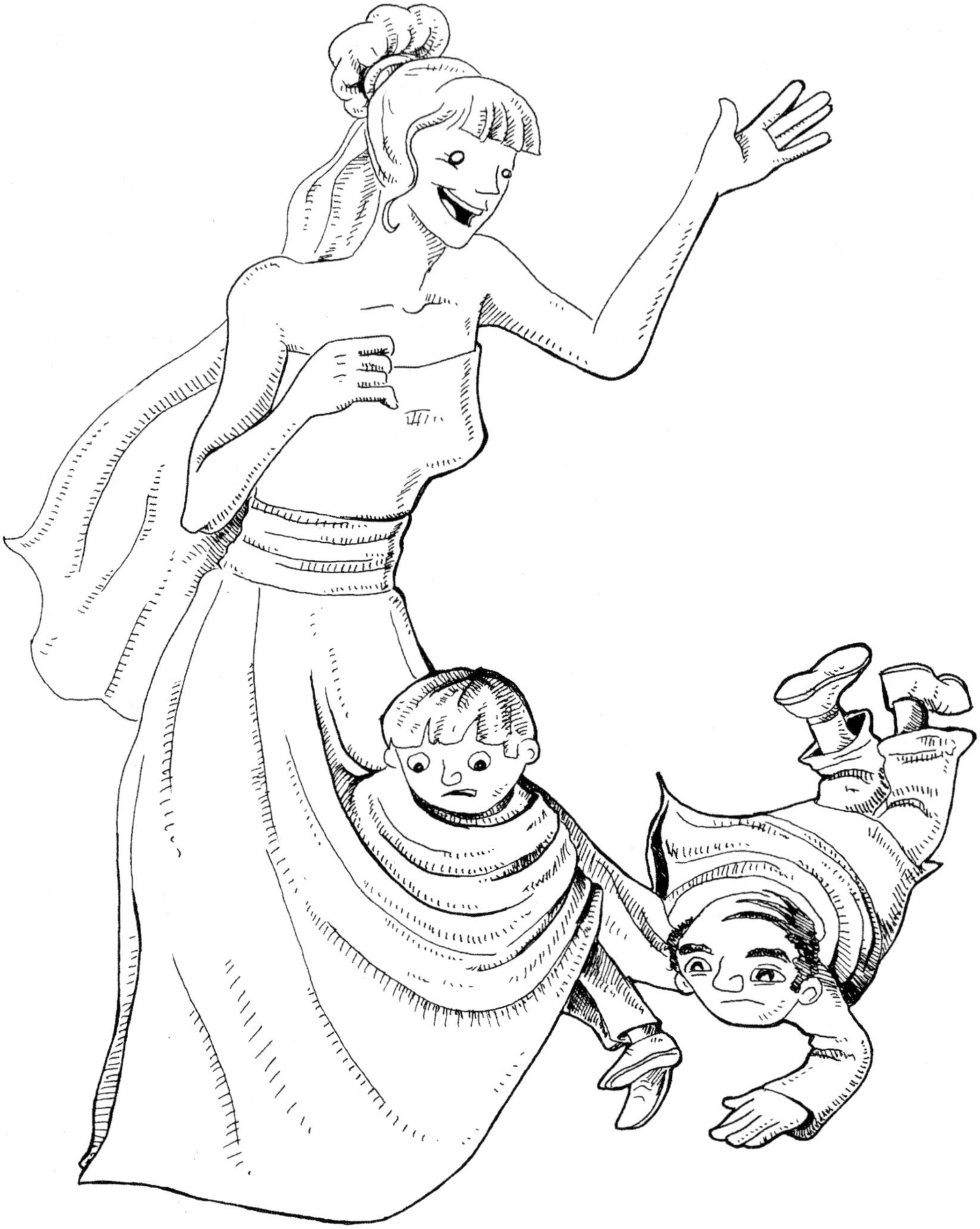

38

DON'T rent a hall without a changing room

Ladies, in particular, will want to have a place other than the restroom to "freshen up" during the reception. A changing room is also nice if you want to get out of your wedding gown when the dancing begins, since wedding and bridesmaids' gowns were not exactly designed with today's "clean" and "family-oriented" dancing techniques in mind.

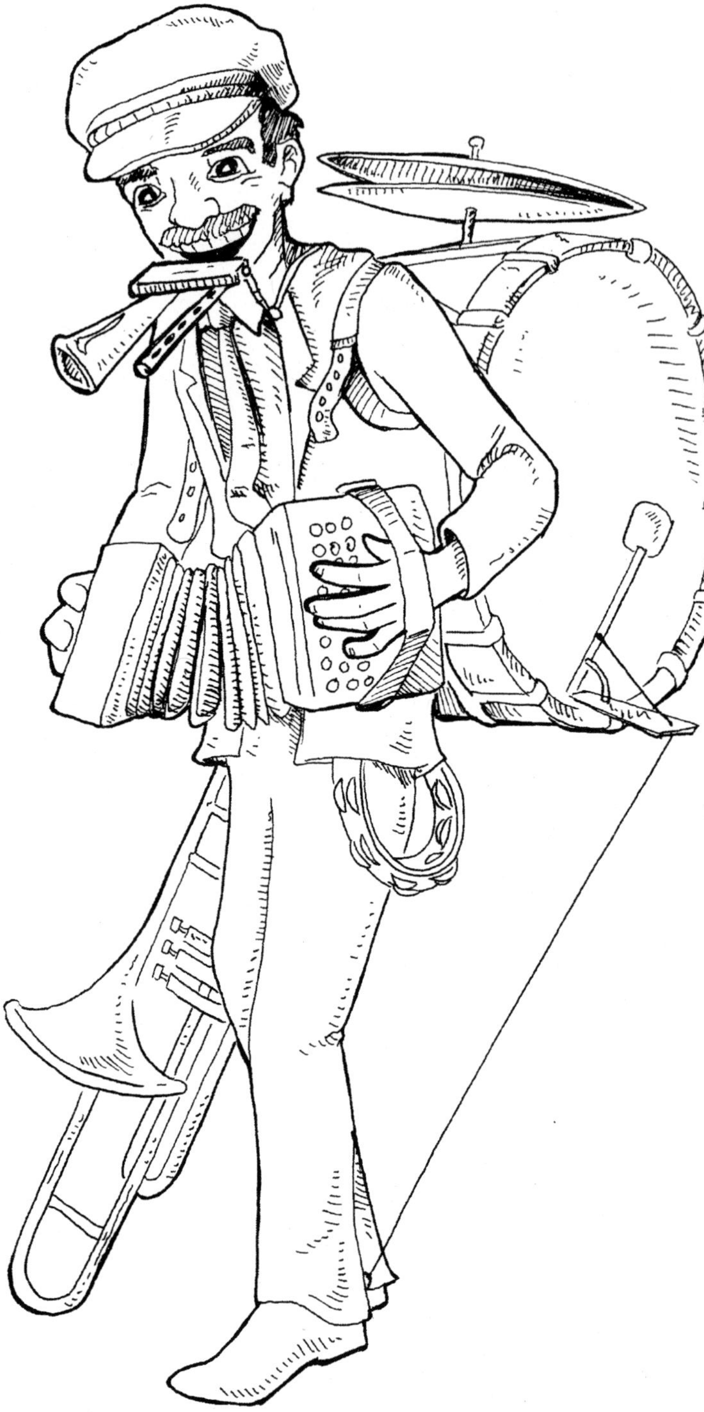

➣ 39 ➣

DON'T hire bad entertainment

We hate to dwell on this, but it is so important to have a good DJ or band at your wedding. Or, hey, be totally different and hire a dueling piano team to perform. That's a great time for everyone! No matter what you choose, the entertainment is the glue to your party. Without good music, your reception will be like spending time alone in a room full of loud, obnoxious drunk people—basically because that is where you are, and that is all you will notice if no one is having a good time.

84

40

DON'T allow intoxicated guests to drive home

Unless you want to deal with the jailing or death of one of your wedding attendees, we suggest you provide transportation home for people who are too drunk to remember their names. We know you are not responsible for anyone's actions, but do a good service here—you did provide the booze and the great party after all. Just make sure everyone makes it home without having to make a stupid decision, other than that pesky decision to drink until a near coma, of course.

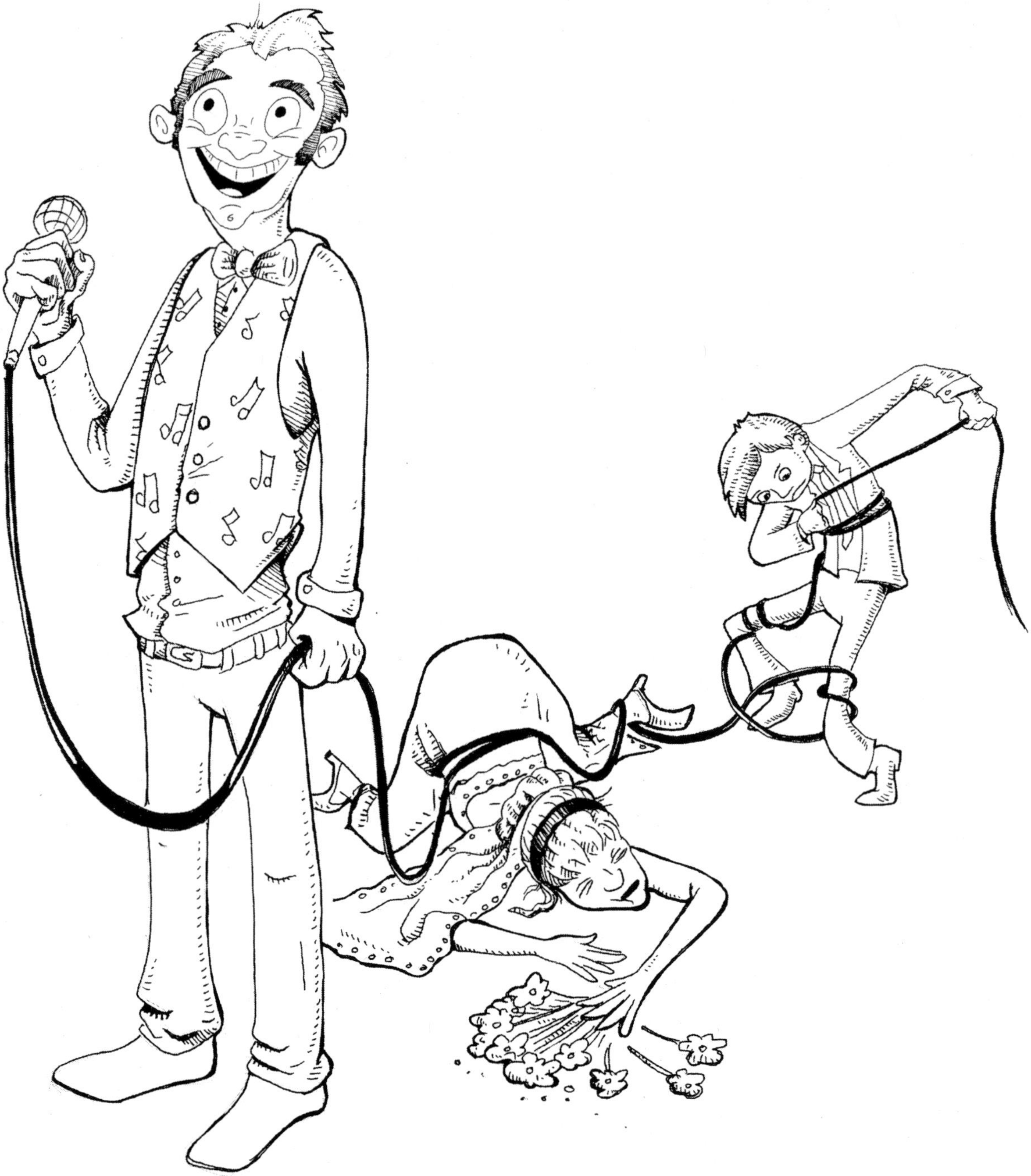

41

DON'T hire a DJ without a wireless microphone

Have you ever seen a bride trip and fall on her ass on the dance floor? That is dangerous. But that is only half of the problem we are dealing with here. The wireless microphone does alleviate the cord problem on the dance floor but really comes into play when preparing and announcing the grand entrance at the reception. Having the MC actually line up your wedding party and announce them from the doorway will ensure the order and name pronunciations are both correct. There is nothing less personal than a DJ butchering the pronunciation of the maid of honor's last name—not such a grand entrance anymore, is it, folks?

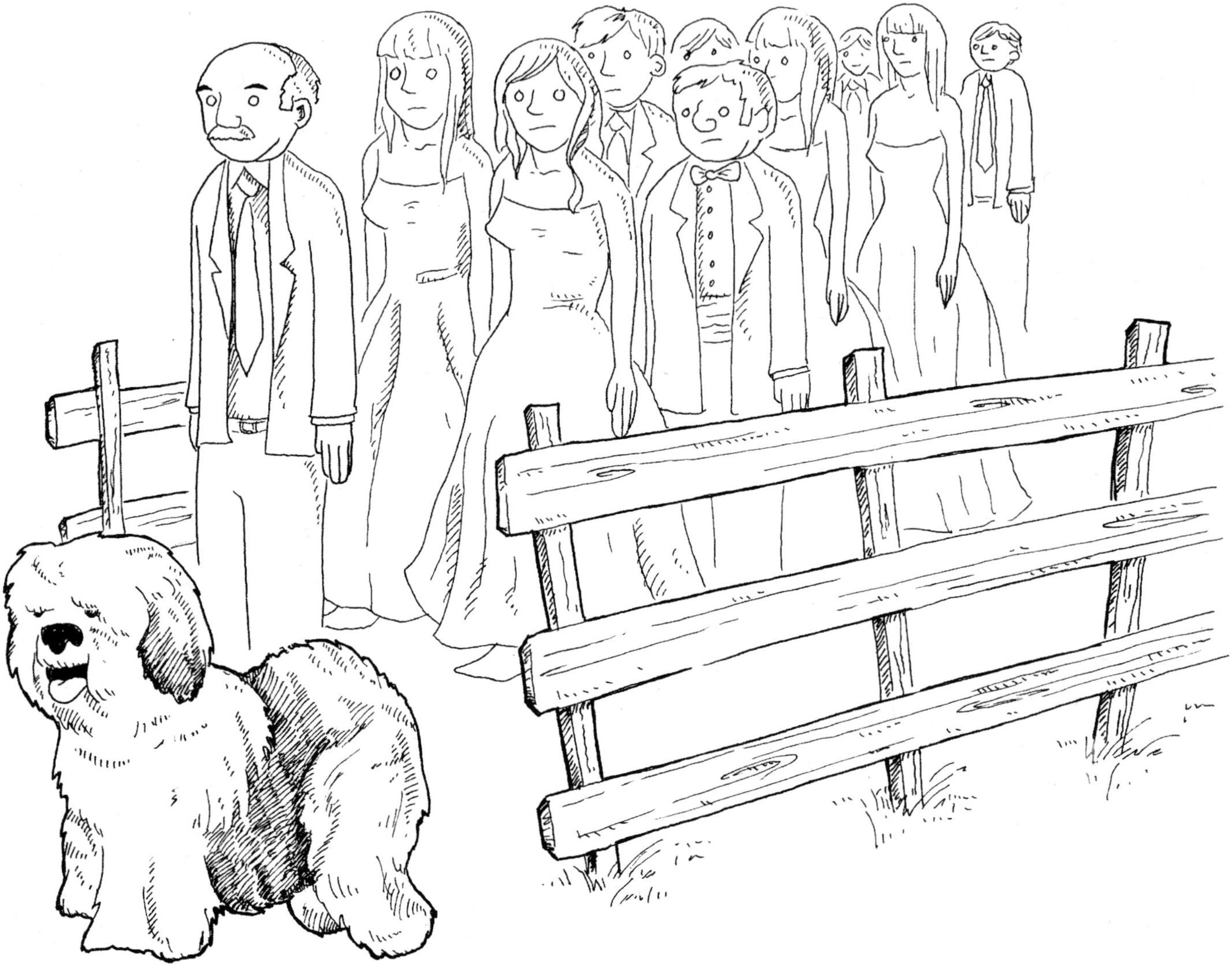

42

DON'T have the cocktail hour far away from the dinner hall

One of the biggest challenges at any event involving masses of people is getting the crowd to migrate anywhere than where they are at the present moment. If you have your cocktail hour in a room that is a distance from the dinner hall, then you're gonna need a dozen sheep dogs to get your guests to move to the dinner table. Keep it close and lose the dogs.

ACTIVITIES TIME STATUS

HAIR AND MAKEUP	3:00	DELAYED
PICTURES	4:00	DELAYED
CEREMONY	5:30	DELAYED
LIMO RIDE	6:30	DELAYED
COCKTAIL HOUR	6:45	DELAYED
ARRIVAL OF PARTY	7:45	DELAYED
DINNER	8:00	DELAYED
DANCING	9:00	DELAYED

43

DON'T operate under a strict itinerary

In well over 100 weddings, we have never been to one that stayed on schedule. Never. Weddings are like airlines—somewhere along the way you are going to be delayed, no matter what carrier you select or how specific you try to plan. And a strict itinerary just makes everyone involved anxious. Cut the stress with broad timelines. They work better and make the day more enjoyable.

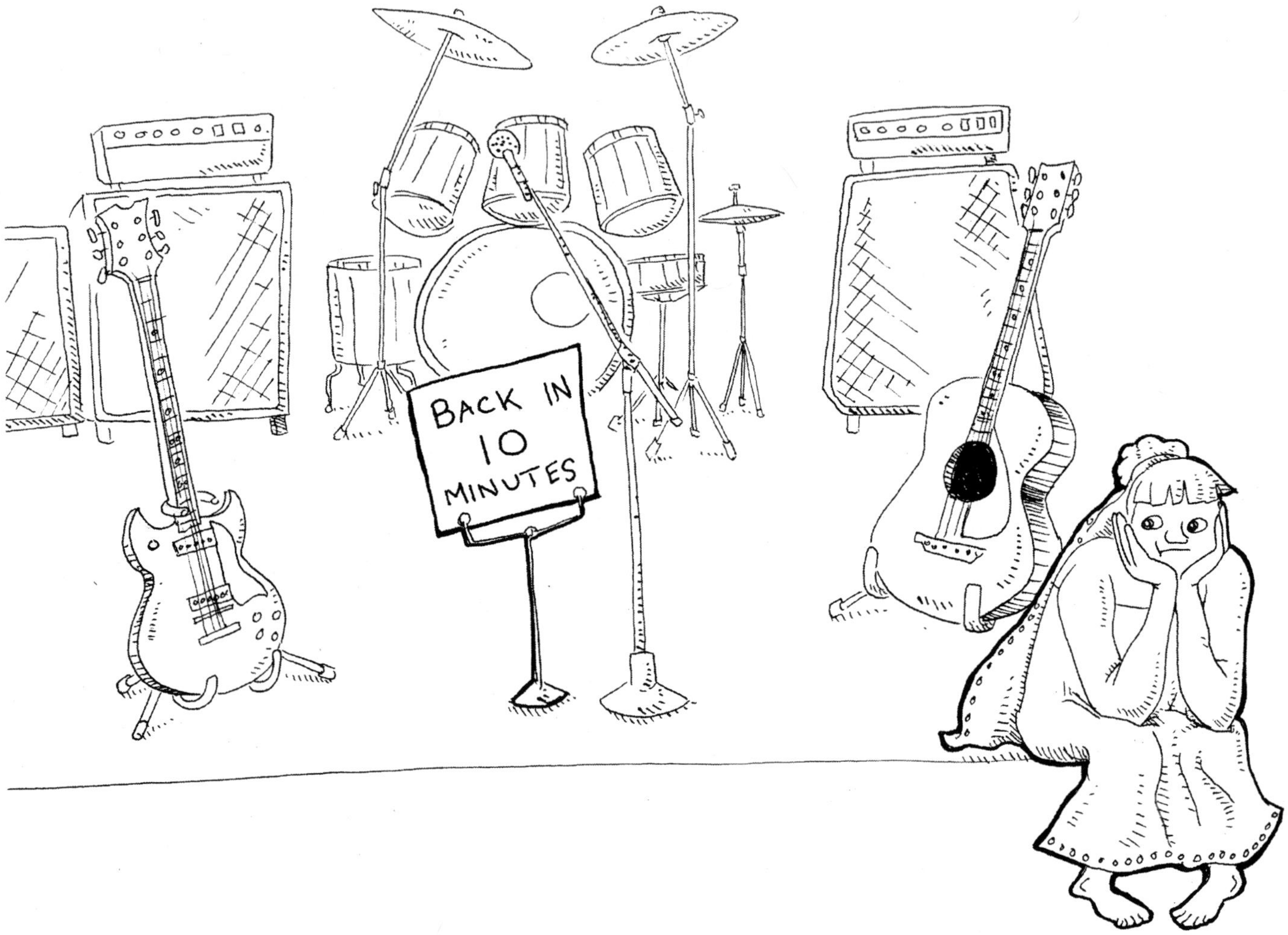
BACK IN
10
MINUTES

44

DON'T allow your band to take breaks

Would you allow the organist at the church to take a smoke break during "The Wedding March"? We think not. Then why would you allow the band to do so in the middle of your awesome party? After all, it's only three hours of playing time you are asking for here. Get a band big enough so that if a few members need to fuel up on nicotine and whiskey shots then the music can still continue. Don't forget, you are paying several thousand dollars for the band's precious three hours. Everyone else has to work the whole time. They should too.

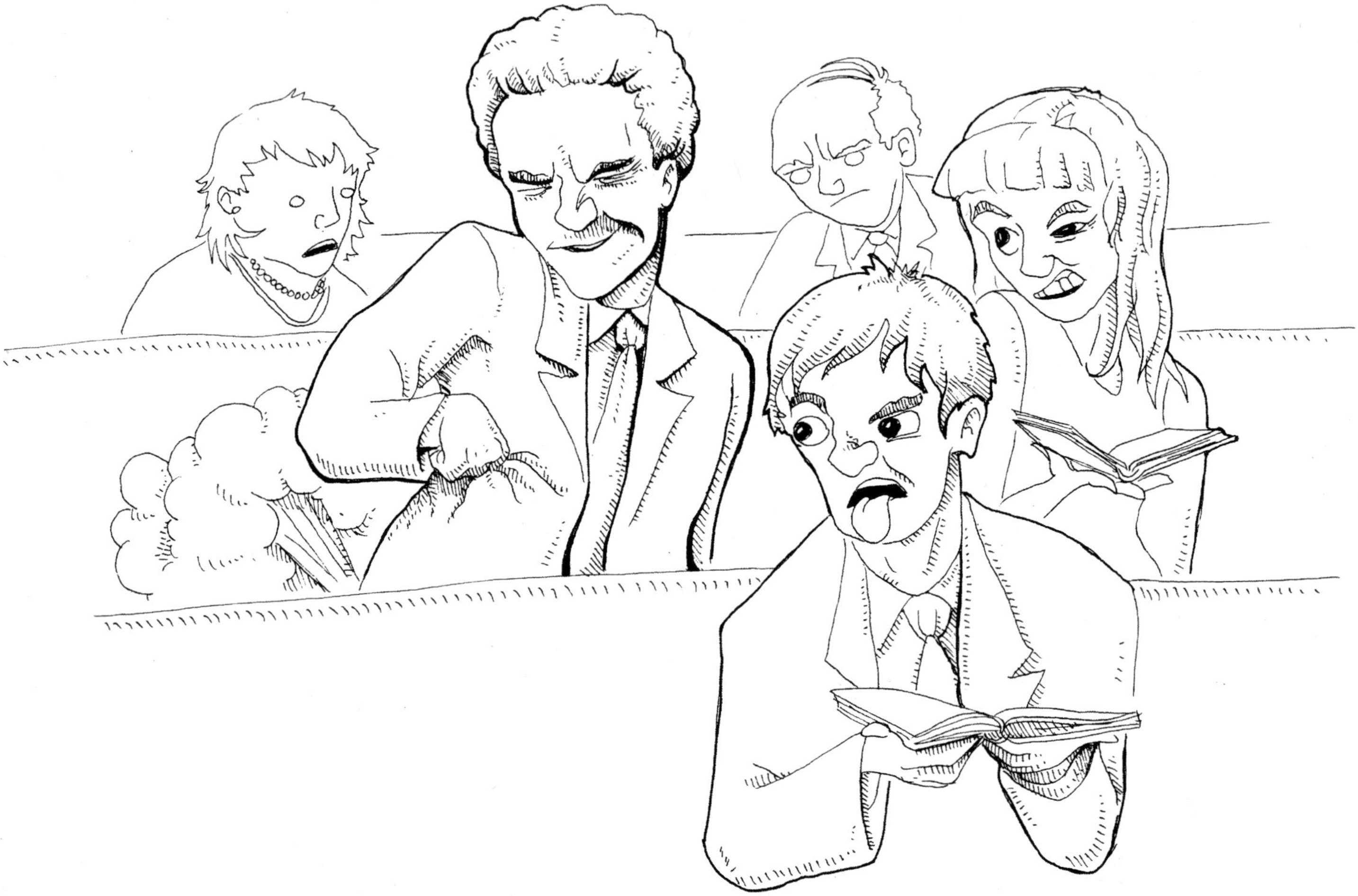

45

DON'T have any downtime during the evening

Downtime at a wedding is like passing some loud gas during a church sermon. It's just really bad. So make sure the evening progresses without any breaks. In case of emergency, let the DJ or band start playing music. A good song can make anyone forget about the stupid, thoughtless toast they just heard.

46

DON'T walk to each table while people wait for the evening to continue

It's great to walk around and say hi to your guests. But by this time of the night, most of your guests are just itchin' to get out there and do the "Electric Slide." Why? We have absolutely no idea. Do not make everyone wait for the tunes to begin for you to get through all 300 people. Just let the DJ or band start playing music while you visit each table. Who cares? You can do the first dance later.

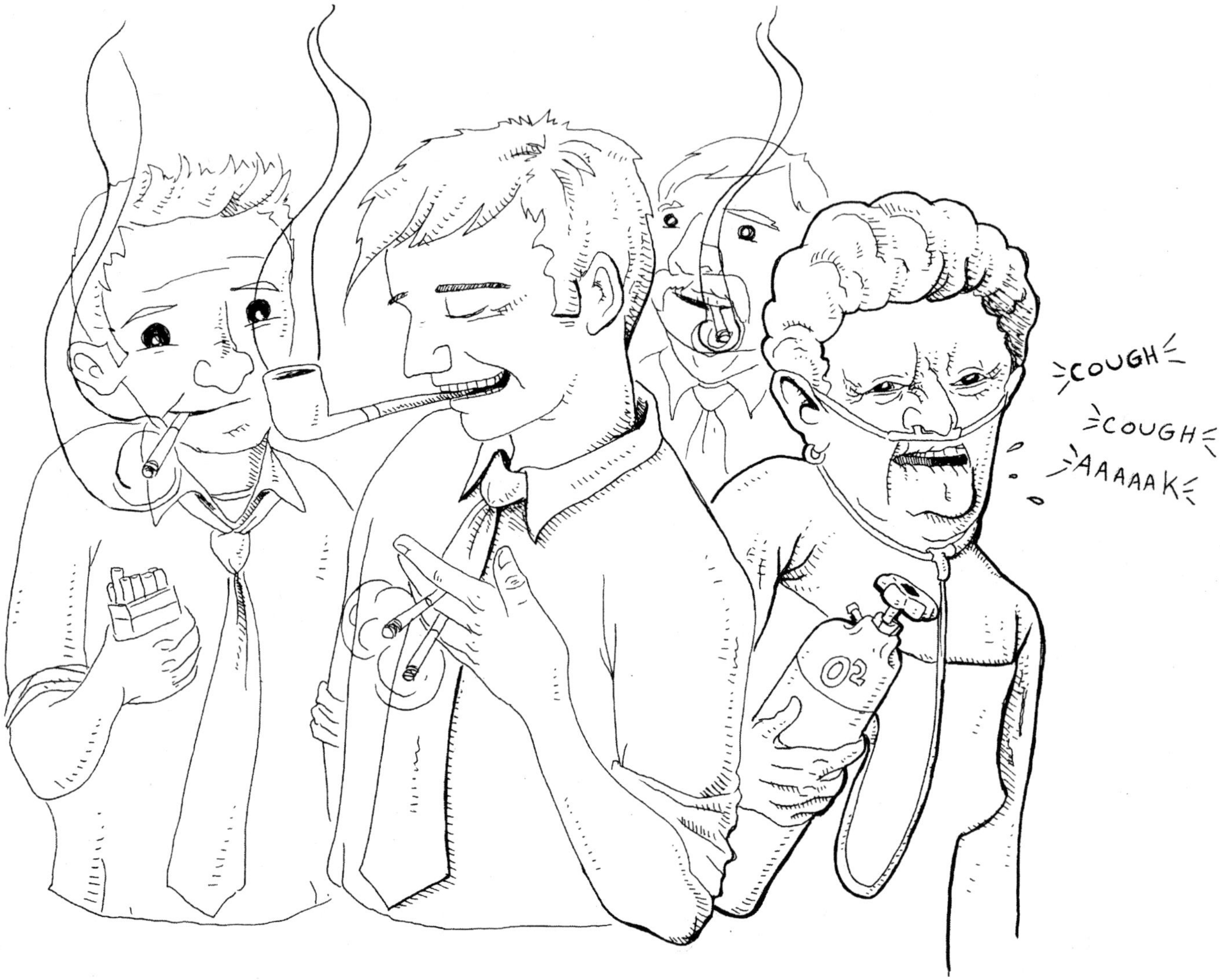

COUGH
COUGH
AAAAAK
O2

47

DON'T allow guests to smoke

Allowing guests to smoke inside is a great idea if you want your reception to end before cocktail hour is over. Face it, smoking around a nonsmoker is like shoving a T-bone down a vegetarian's throat. Smokers know that they belong outside. So, make them go out in the tar jungle and mingle with the other nicotine dwellers.

100

48

DON'T let your caterer rush the meal

Isn't it annoying when you are at a restaurant and your entrees arrive during the appetizer or salad course? Now you have both a giant bloomin' onion and a 24-ounce porterhouse to tackle before they both get cold. Meals are rushed usually because the food is sitting in the back getting cold—no big surprise there. But this is totally avoidable if the caterer uses a secret technique called "good timing." Of course, you do not want cold food, but you do need to allow enough time for your guests to enjoy each course. A 2-hour meal is a bit too long, and a 45-minute one is entirely too short. Try to stick with around 90 minutes for your dinner.

SUPER AWESOME DJ SOUNDS
UPCOMING GIGS
May
S M T W T F S
1 2 3 4 5
6 7 8 9 10 11 12
13 14 15 16 17 18 19
20 21 22 23 24 25 26
27 28 29 30 31

49

DON'T book entertainment without previewing first in person

Once you have narrowed it down to a couple choices for your entertainment, plan a Saturday night to drive around and check them out in action. Have fun, dress up, and make a date out of it with your fiancé. Here's a tip - if your entertainment has no gigs booked for you to view, then they probably suck.

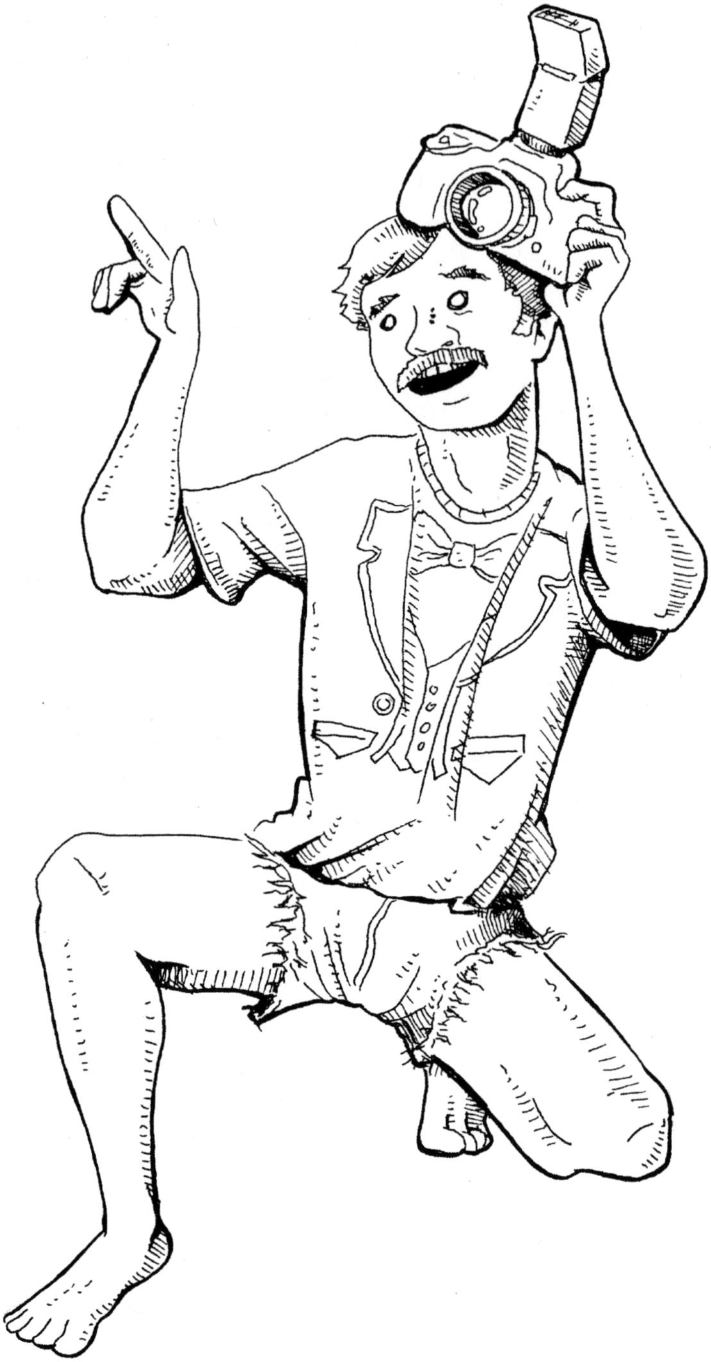

50

DON'T allow your vendors to dress as they please

Without a dress code, do not be surprised if you see a vendor in jean shorts and a tuxedo-print T-shirt. No, really, we are serious. Specify the dress code before the wedding.

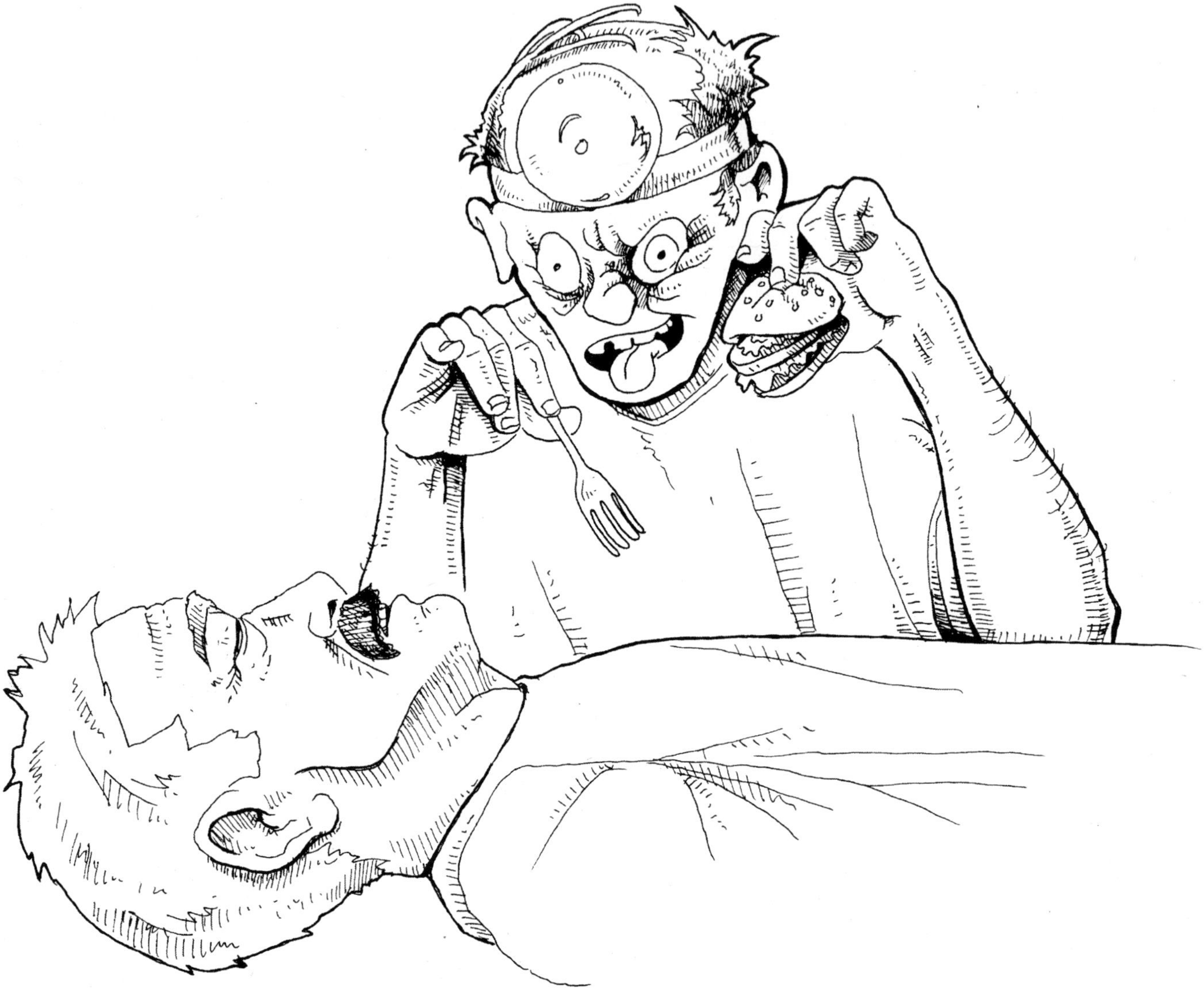

51

DON'T select the meal without a tasting

Don't spend $10,000 or more on a meal that you have not sampled. That is like agreeing to an experimental surgery before confirming that you are actually dealing with a real doctor. Go taste the food. It's free. You might end up making some changes once you realize that you do not want shaved almonds on your green beans after all.

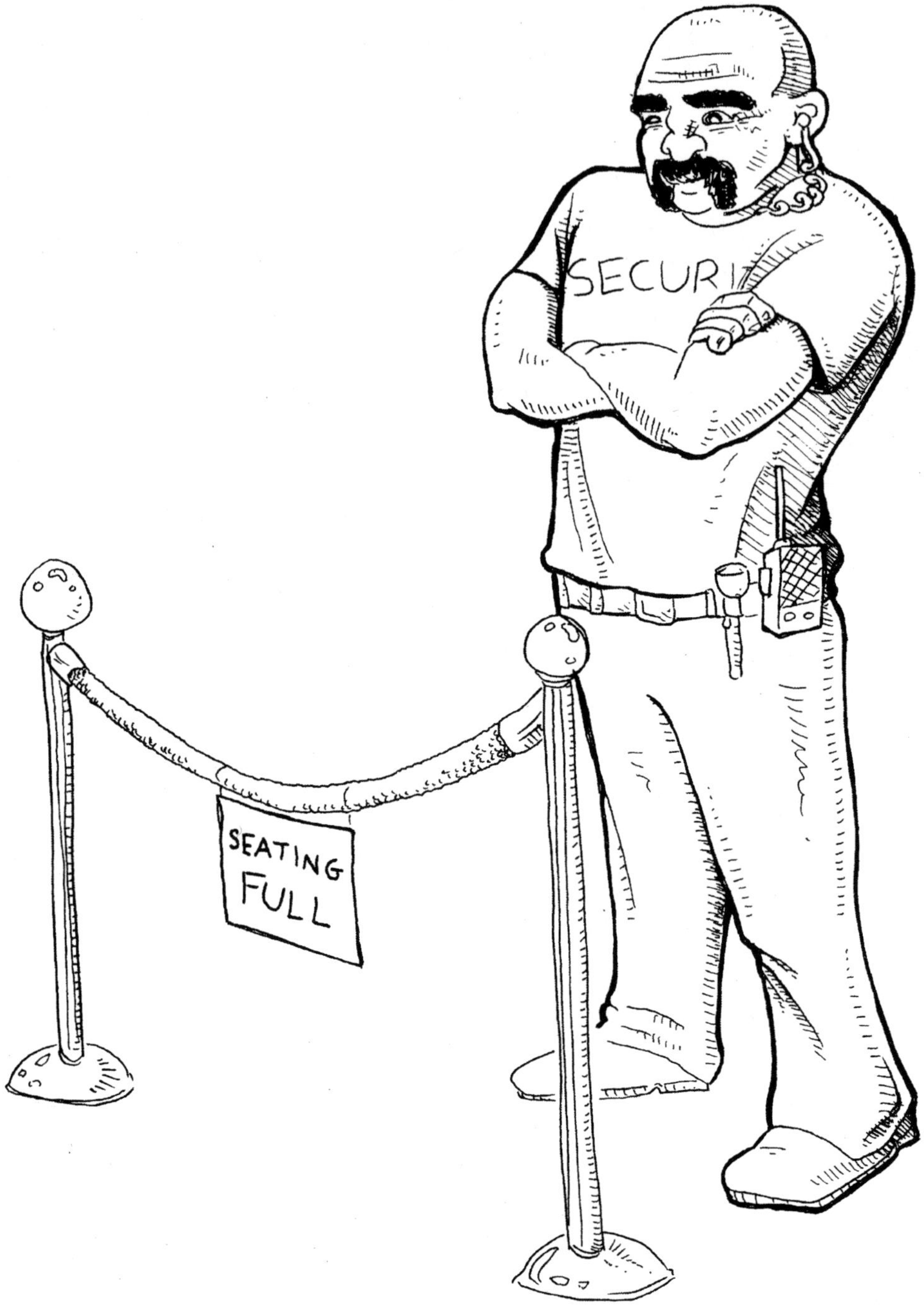
SECURI
SEATING
FULL

52

DON'T forget the seating chart

Your banquet coordinator will most likely tell you that a seating chart is not necessary. This is because they are lazy and do not want to add extra work for themselves. Remember, you are just one of many, many weddings they have over the course of the year. Many coordinators say that up to 10 percent of the people you invite will not show up. But to get rid of all that extra seating is a bad idea. You are paying for those guests' seats whether they show up or not—so keep 'em out there. A seating chart is very necessary and is well worth the time involved. You can make sure everyone has a seat by controlling who sits where and that there will be ample space for everyone.

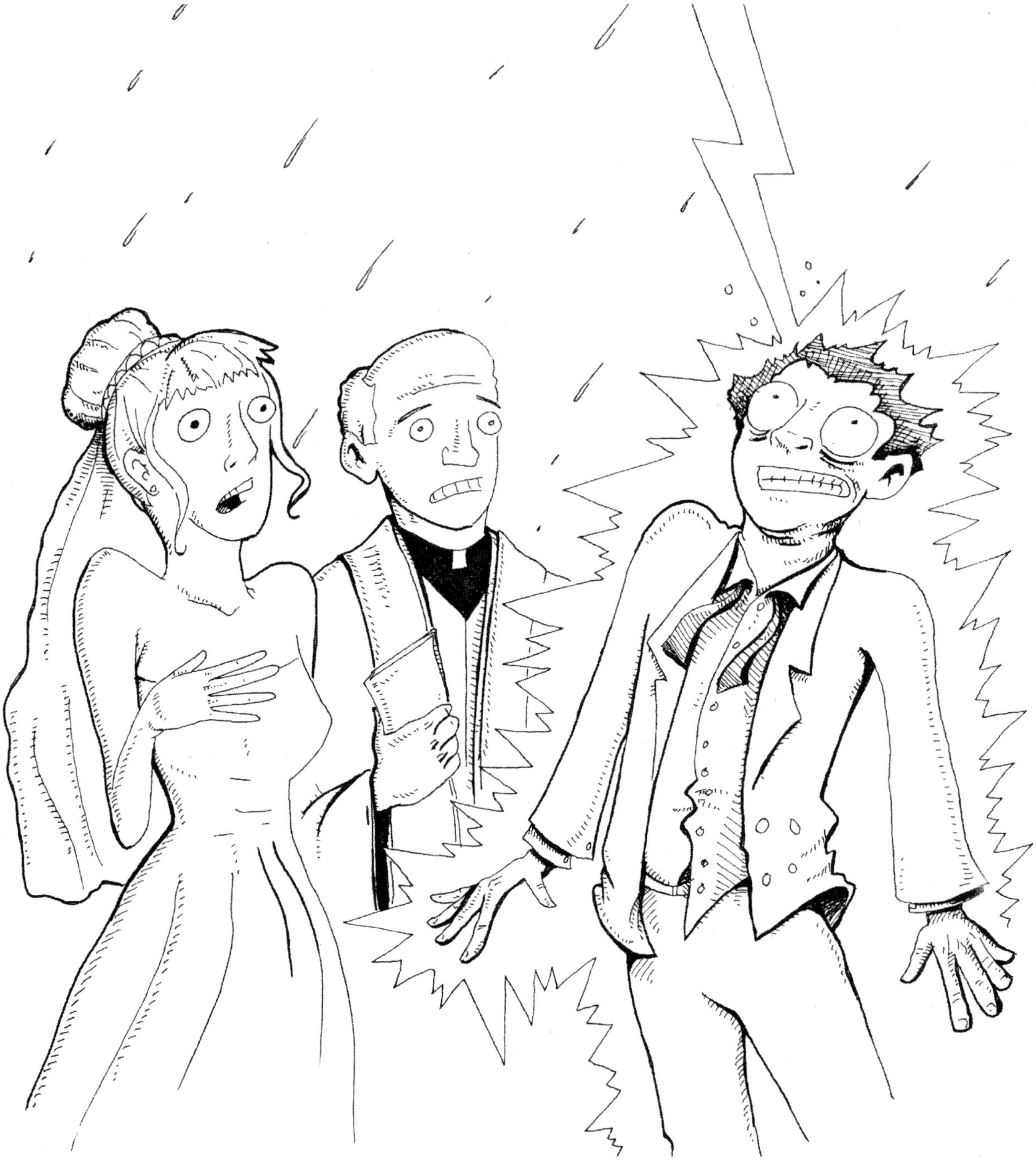

53

DON'T have an outdoor wedding

With the right weather, having an outdoor wedding can be an awesome experience. With the wrong weather, having an outdoor wedding can be like having a colonoscopy without drugs. With all the other details that could go wrong at your wedding, why risk having to deal with intense heat, frigid air, or an extreme downpour? It is just not worth it.

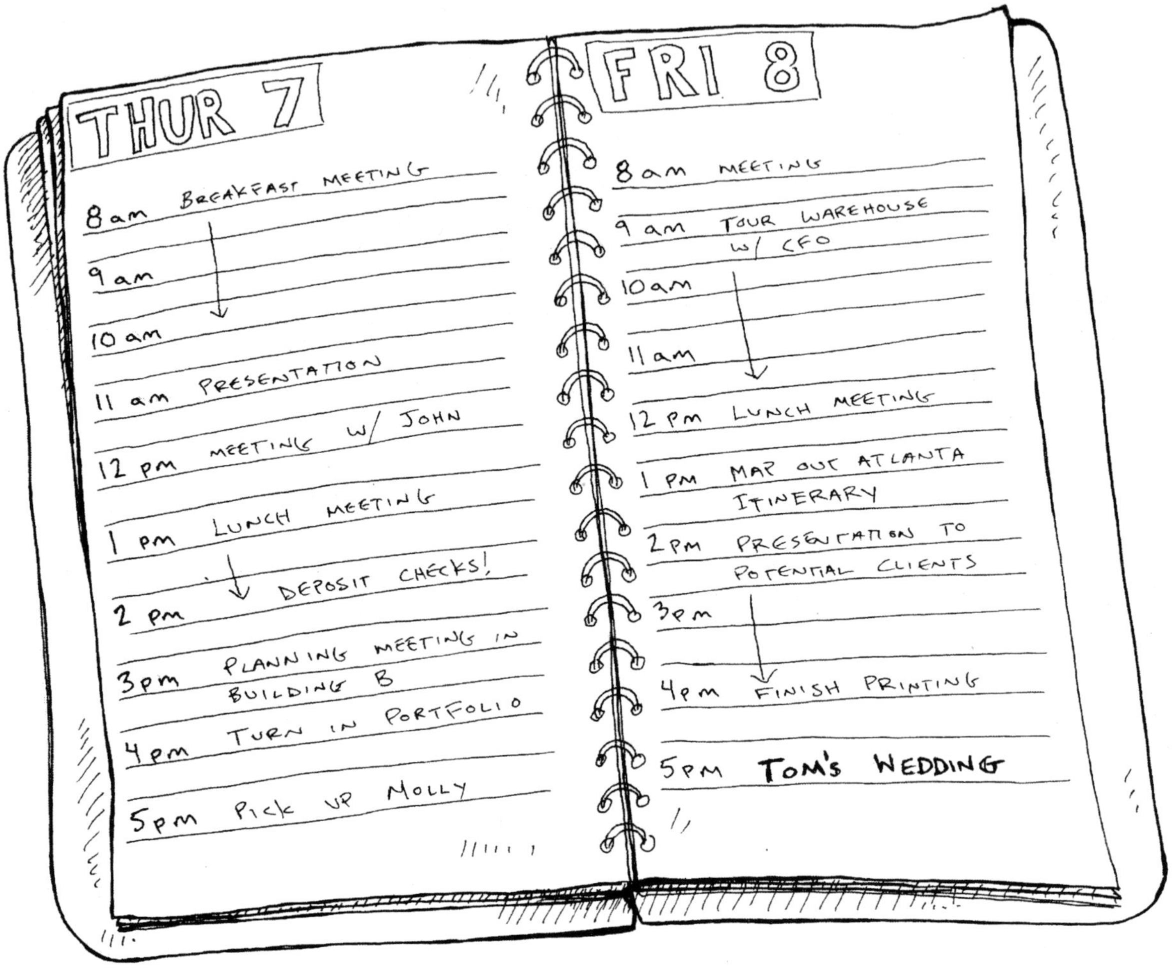
THUR 7
8am BREAKFAST MEETING
9am
10 am
11 am PRESENTATION
12 pm MEETING W/ JOHN
1 pm LUNCH MEETING
DEPOSIT CHECKS!
2 pm
3pm PLANNING MEETING IN BUILDING B
4pm TURN IN PORTFOLIO
5pm PICK UP MOLLY
FRI 8
8am MEETING
9am TOUR WAREHOUSE W/ CFO
10am
11am
12pm LUNCH MEETING
1pm MAP OUT ATLANTA ITINERARY
2pm PRESENTATION TO POTENTIAL CLIENTS
3pm
4pm FINISH PRINTING
5pm TOM'S WEDDING

54

DON'T have a Friday night wedding

Welcome to Earth—the home of your guests. On Earth, people work for a living. Fridays on Earth always have been and always will be workdays. Thank you.

While Friday night weddings might be a bit cheaper, they actually are much harder on your guests. These folks are just finishing up long stressful weeks at work and need the night to relax with their families—not to get all dressed up to go to a wedding. If you are that strapped for cash, we suggest you reduce your guest list or cut out some luxury items, such as the limo, the expensive cake, and excessive flowers, and go with a Saturday date.

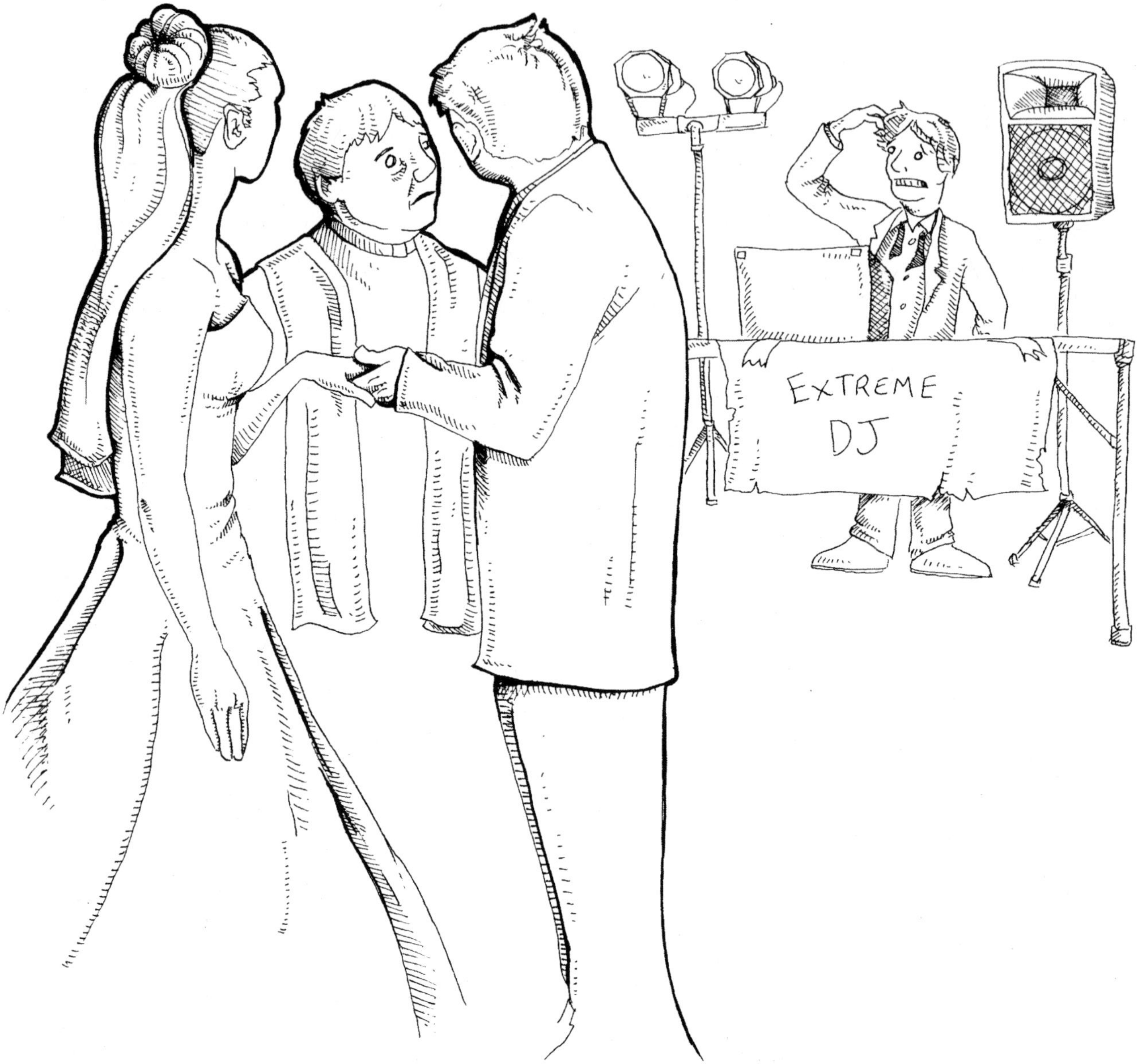
EXTREME
DJ

55

DON'T have the DJ provide music at your ceremony

How much are you spending on your wedding? $10,000? $30,000? $50,000? Wow! Get rid of a floral arrangement and invest $200 for a pianist, or a harpist, to play during the ceremony. It is quite a sight to see the DJ in a corner, cueing up a prerecorded version of "The Wedding March." And when the CD accidentally skips, well, that's quite a sight as well.

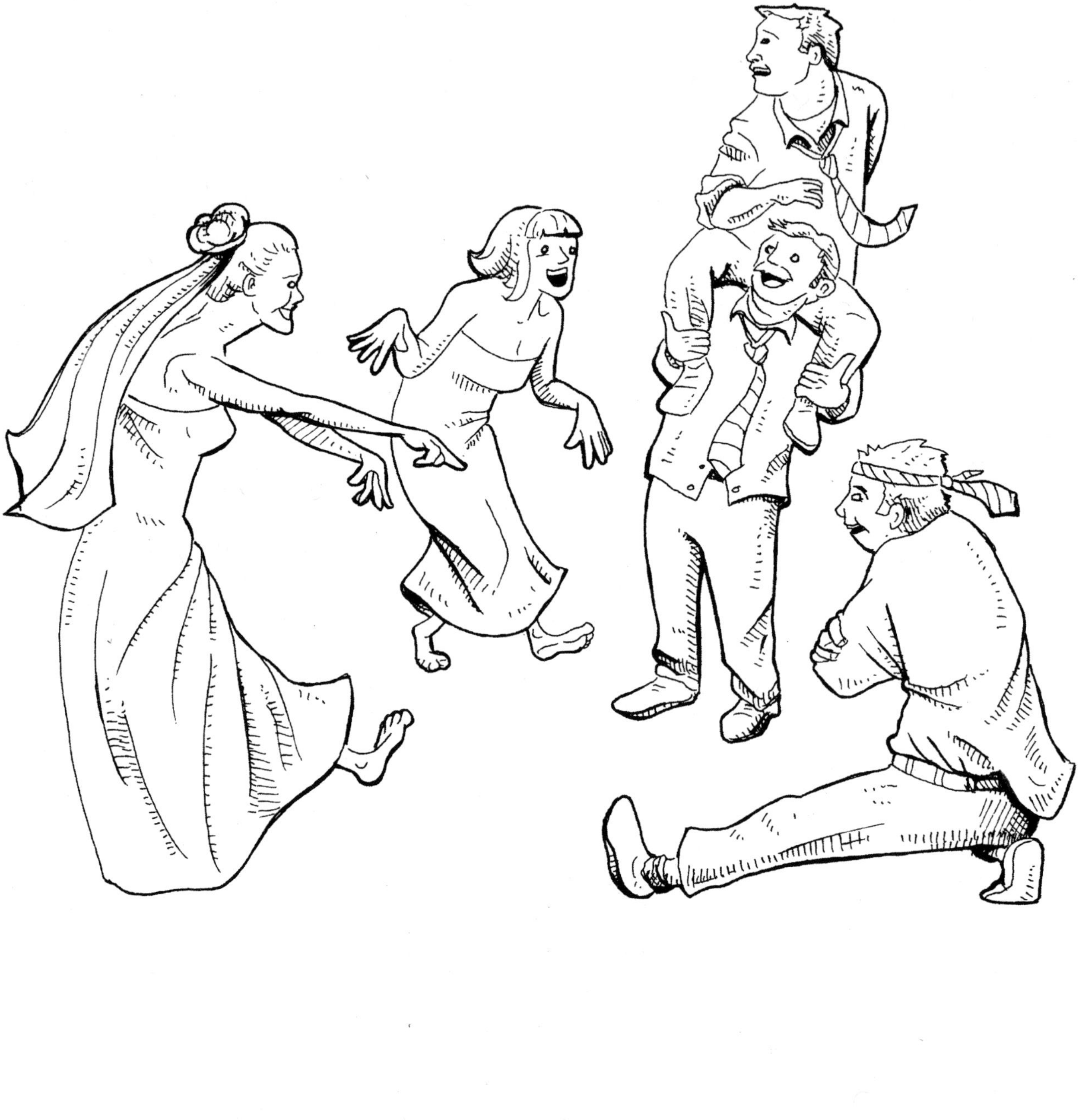

56

DON'T exceed 3.5 hours for postdinner dancing

Three and a half hours should just about cover it for the postdinner dancing. After this amount of time, the "sloppy drunk syndrome" will surely set in, if it hasn't already, and you will be in store for eventual problems. This, my friends, is a mathematical certainty. All you have to do is add up the shots and drinks consumed by your friends and family. End it on a high note, just after midnight, and let the hotel, police department, and animal control deal with your crazy guests from there.

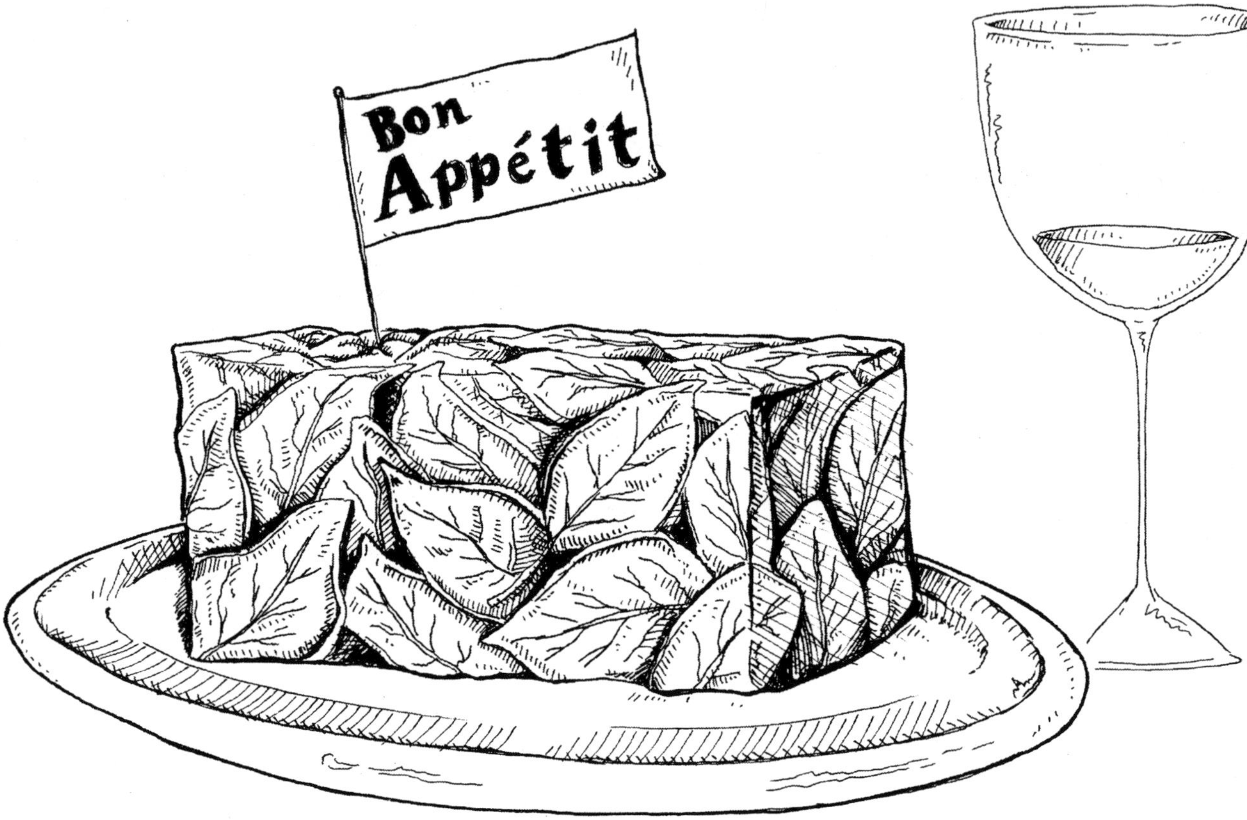
Bon
Appétit

57

DON'T have a vegetarian meal only

This goes back to our philosophy that you need to think about your guests. While we are sure they appreciate your love for animals and nature, most will not want to partake in your nonmeat eating habits. Our good friend spent a fortune on a fancy vegetarian dinner only to end up with a ton of wasted tofu and greens and a lot of hungry unsatisfied guests. Don't try to convert your guests. Offer a selection—or waste a lot of money. It's your choice.

58

DON'T select music only according to your tastes

We know we have said it over and over again, but your wedding is about you and your guests. So remember them when selecting your music choices. Let your DJ or band read the crowd. If you hired good talent, then he will do a great job at selecting the best music at the right times to maximize a dancing and party-like atmosphere. Just be open-minded here—get your favorite tunes in there, of course, but make sure your guests can make requests, too. Oh yeah, one quick suggestion: Never ever play, "The Macarena," at your wedding—or anywhere else. Ever.

122

59

DON'T worry about the time all night

Stop worrying about everything. Your wedding night is going to go by so fast you will not believe it when it's over. You did a good job planning—now it is time for you to have fun, enjoy the night, and let the people you hired make it happen. We are sure they are competent people—right?

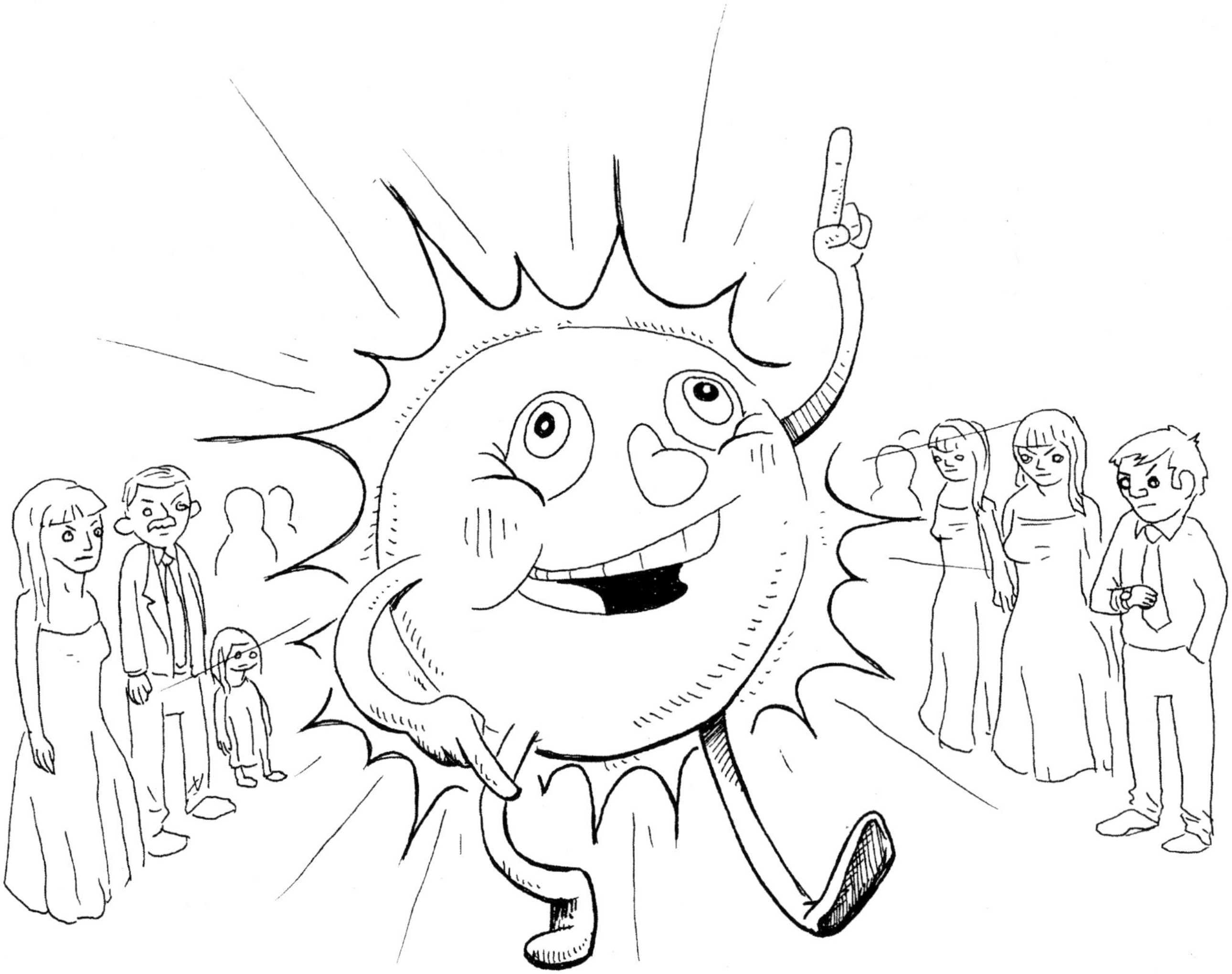

60

DON'T start your reception too early

Starting your reception at 3:00 PM or 4:00 PM is just too early. By the time dinner is over, it is not even dark yet. It's hard to get a good dance party going at 6:30 PM. The best schedule is as follows: Cocktail Hour from 5:30 to 7:00 PM; Dinner from 7:30 to 9:00 PM; and Dancing and Fun until 12:30 AM.

"Hey Amy. Just wondering if you have a block of rooms at any nearby hotels. Jenny called and asked and I wasnt sure. So I told her to give you a call too. Eric also asked the other night but....."

61

DON'T make guests find their own hotel rooms

You are no travel agent, but do a service here and provide out of town guests with a block of rooms at a nearby hotel. Otherwise, you'll have to deal with out of town guests calling and asking you: "Hey, do you have a block of rooms at a nearby hotel?"

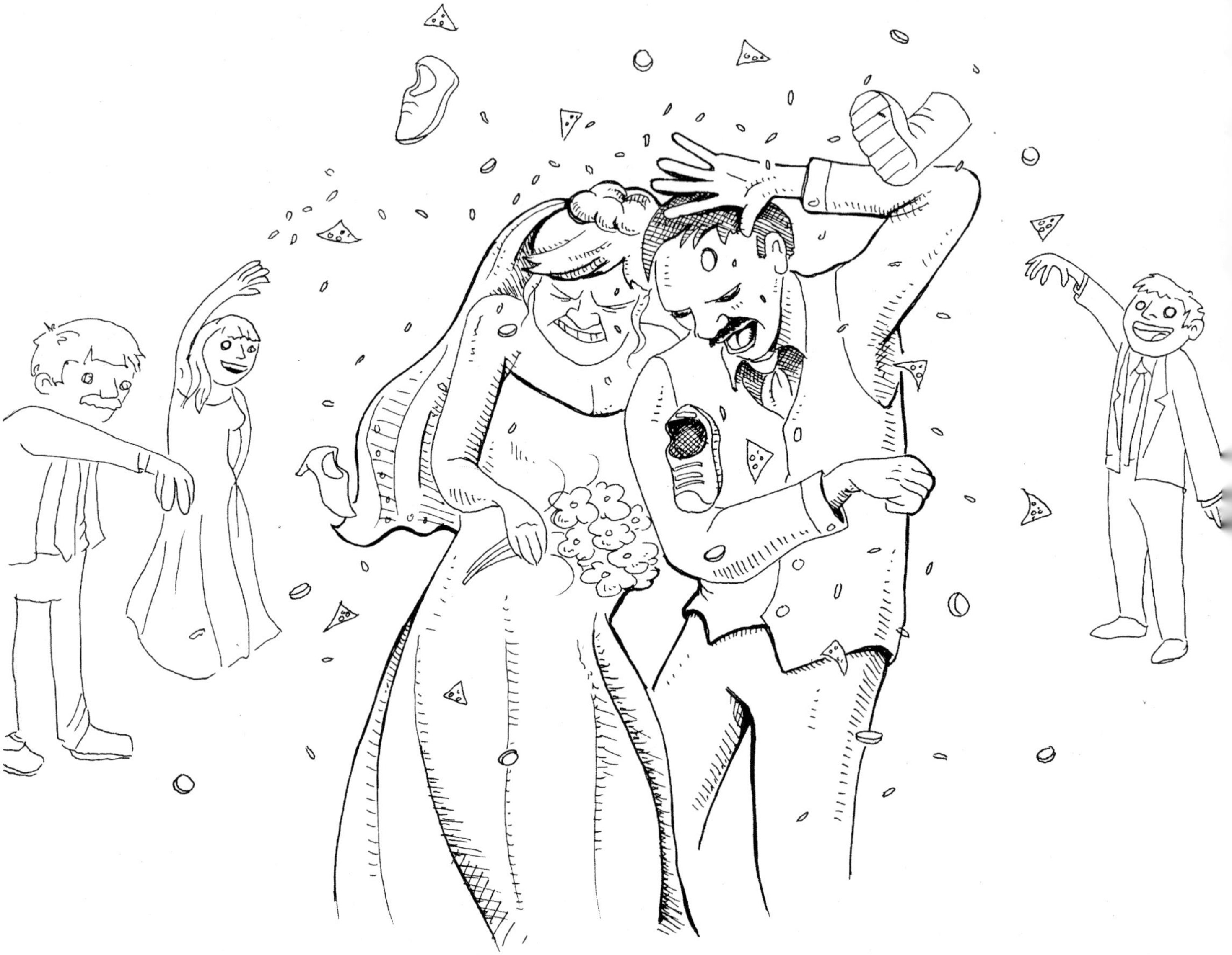

62

DON'T let guests throw rice at you

Do your friends throw marbles at you when you get home from work? Probably not. Then why do you want people throwing rice at you when you leave the church? Why not let them throw coins at you? At least money is useful. Hey, how about chips and salsa? There's nothing like a good snack after a long ceremony. No, we got it - just let your guests throw their shoes at you when you walk out. Everyone needs shoes. We were raised to believe that throwing things at people is not nice. So come on—let's stop throwing rice at the people we care about on their special day. It's stupid and nobody likes it. And frankly, it's just a waste of perfectly good rice. Oh yeah, bubbles suck too.

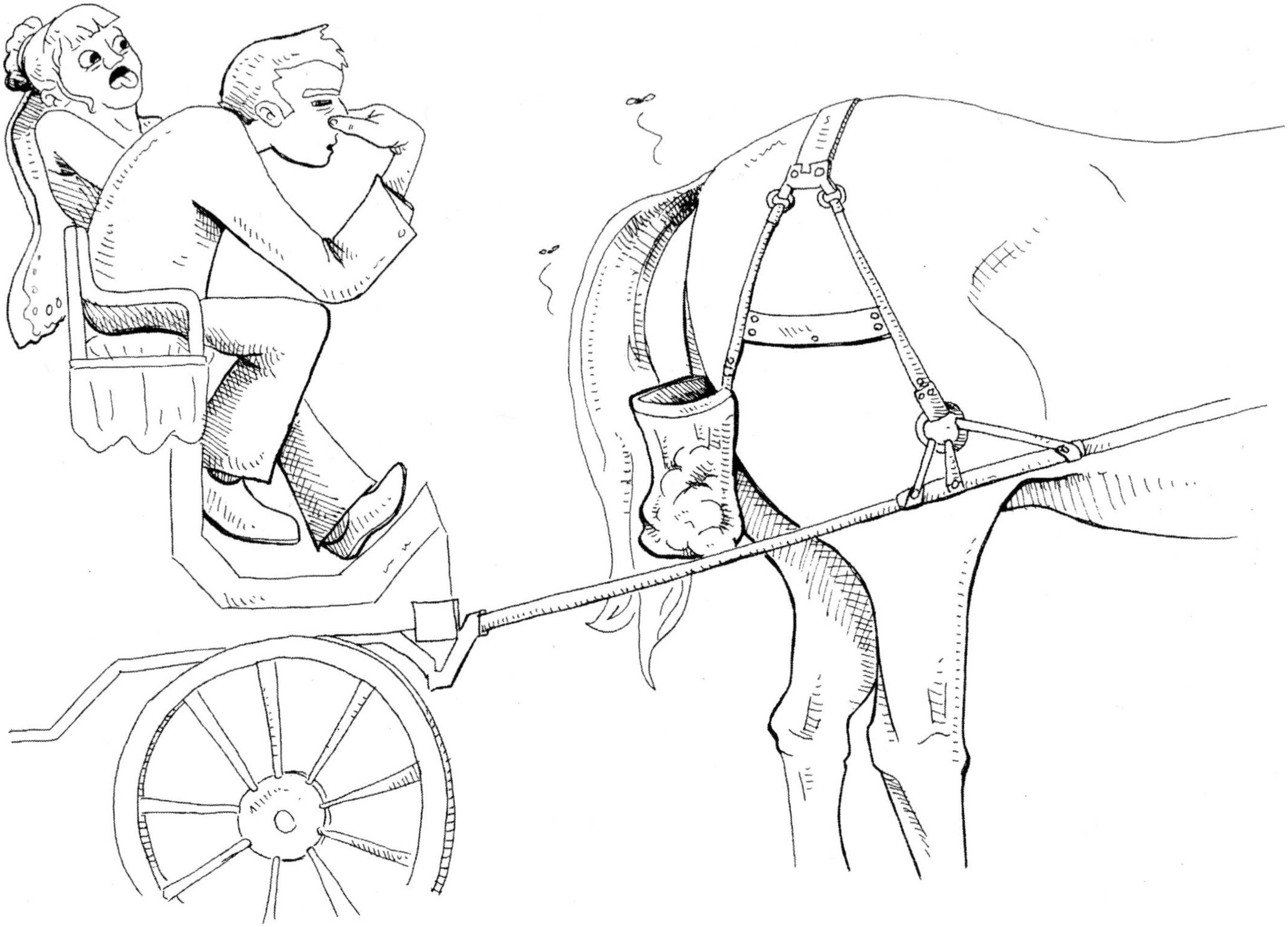

63

DON'T get a horse and carriage

The carriage might be nice and romantic, but the horse taking a crap less than five feet from your face is not.

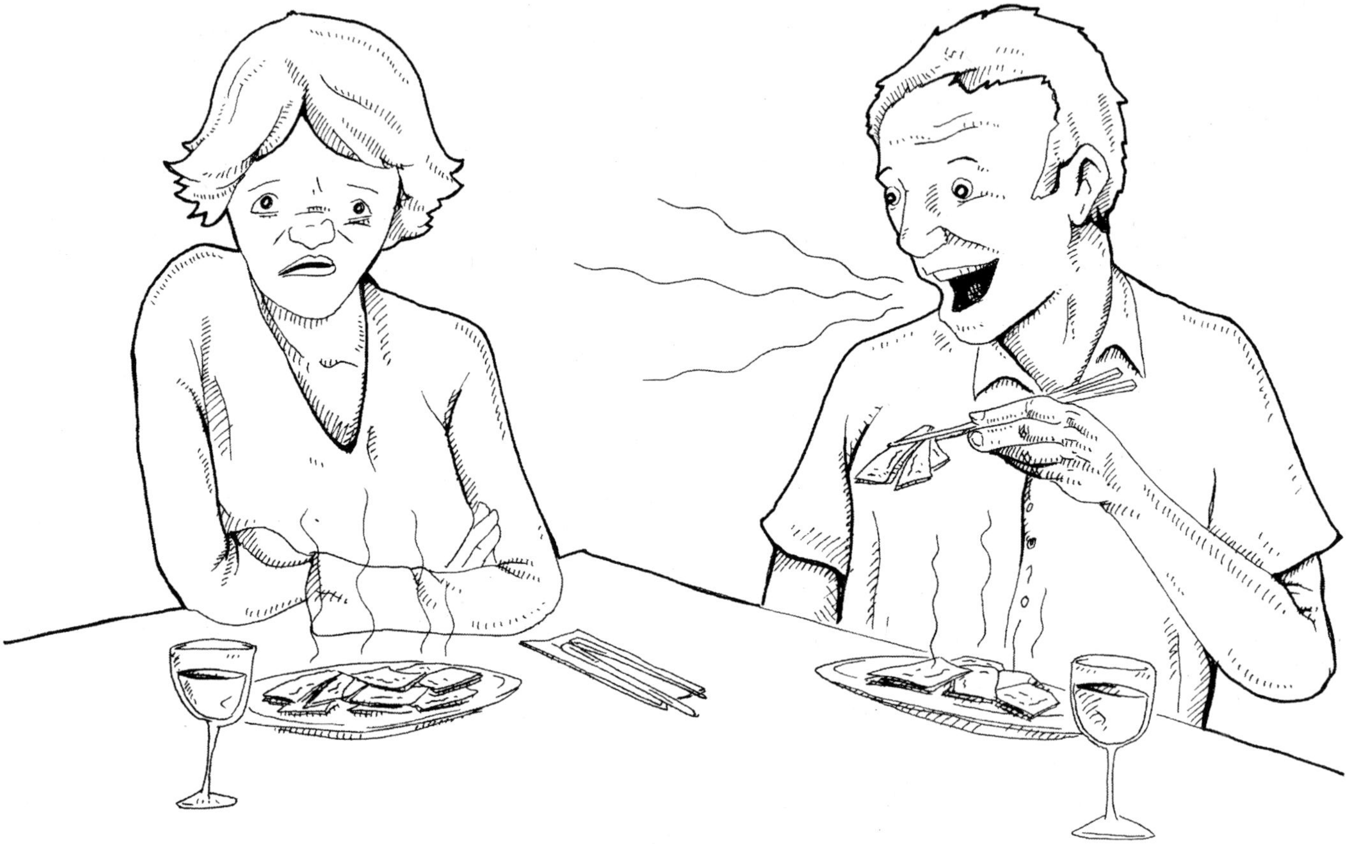

64

DON'T hire a DJ company without meeting your DJ

It is so important to research and meet your DJ. So important. Do not hire a company just based on a recommendation. We know it may seem easy, and you will be glad to have it over with, but really hiring just on a recommendation is like going on a blind date. A good friend might have set you up, but that does not mean your friend knows that your date has a secret pickled cabbage fetish. Get out there and watch the DJ in person beforehand—and feel confident that you are making the right decision.

∞ 65 ∞

DON'T have a super long train

Super long trains get stepped on. A lot. And when this happens, brides tend to fall over and get mad.

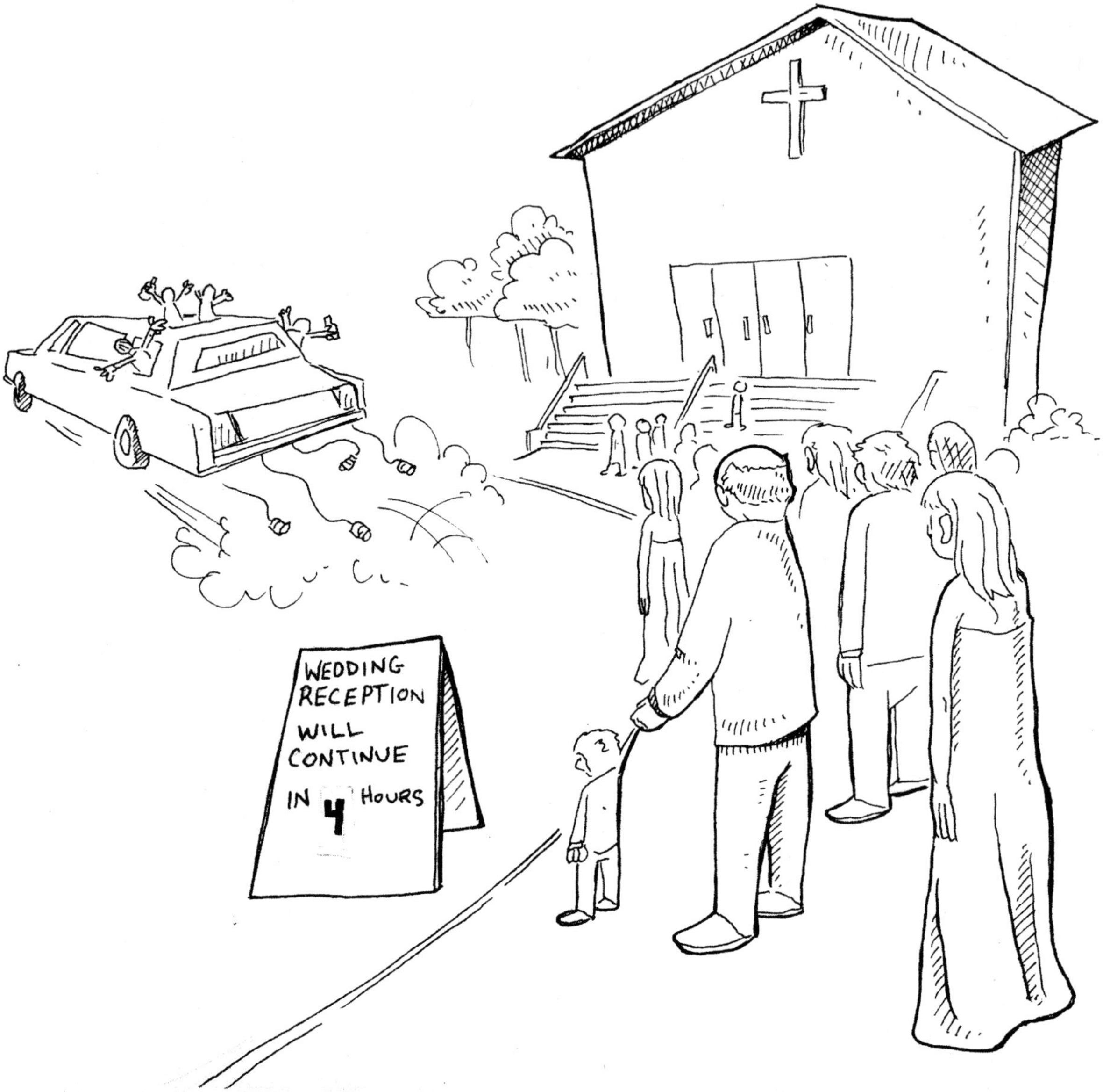
WEDDING
RECEPTION
WILL
CONTINUE
IN 4 HOURS

∽ 66 ∾

DON'T have a lot of time in between the wedding and reception

Plan enough time for travel in between the ceremony and reception, but keep the party moving. Your guests, especially those from out of town, have nothing else to do. So at least let them grab a drink and relax at the reception hall while they wait for you to drink twenty bottles of cheap champagne with your bridal party in an overpriced limousine.

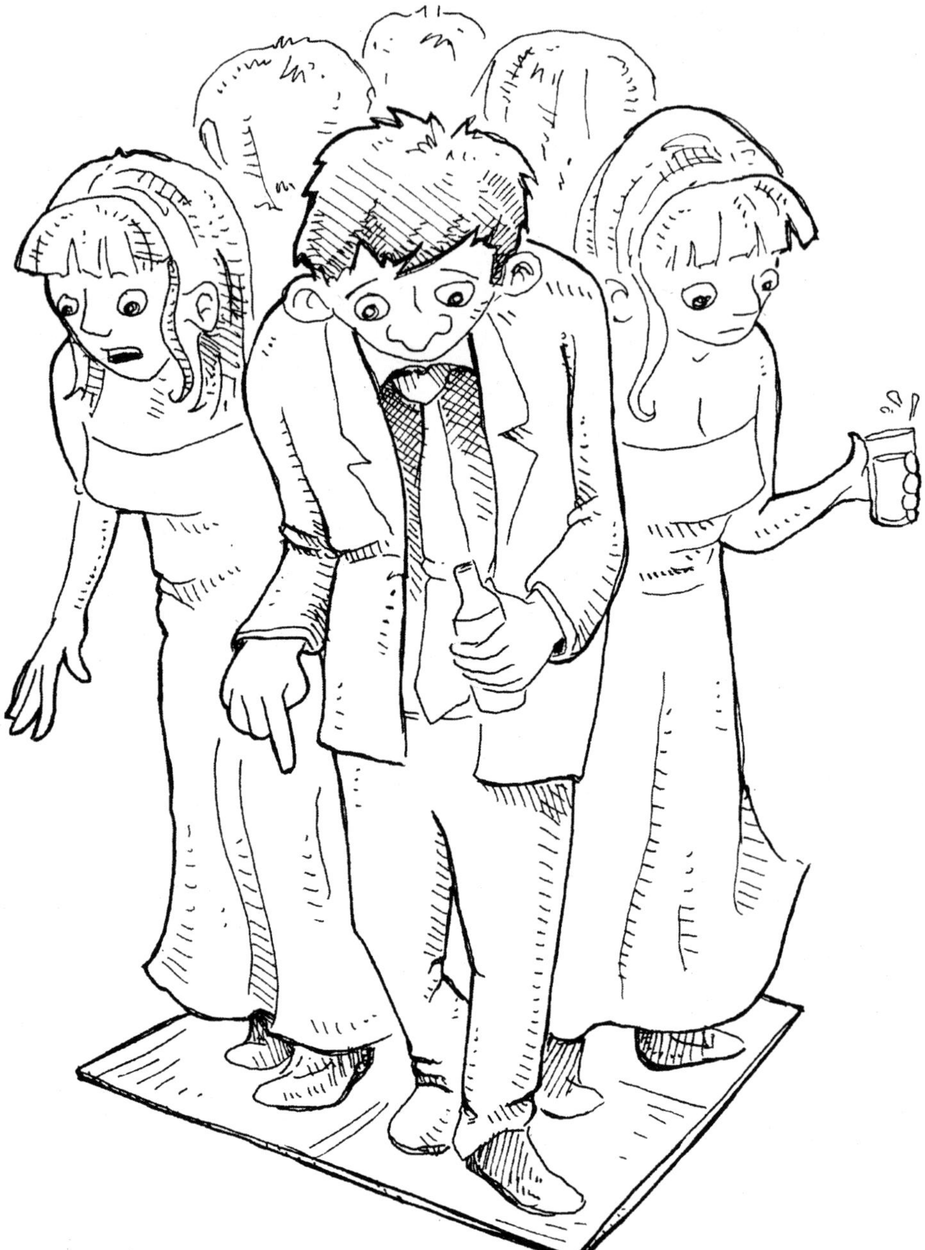

67

DON'T have a small dance floor

This is pretty self-explanatory, but very important. Make sure your dance floor is actually big enough to accommodate more than ten people.

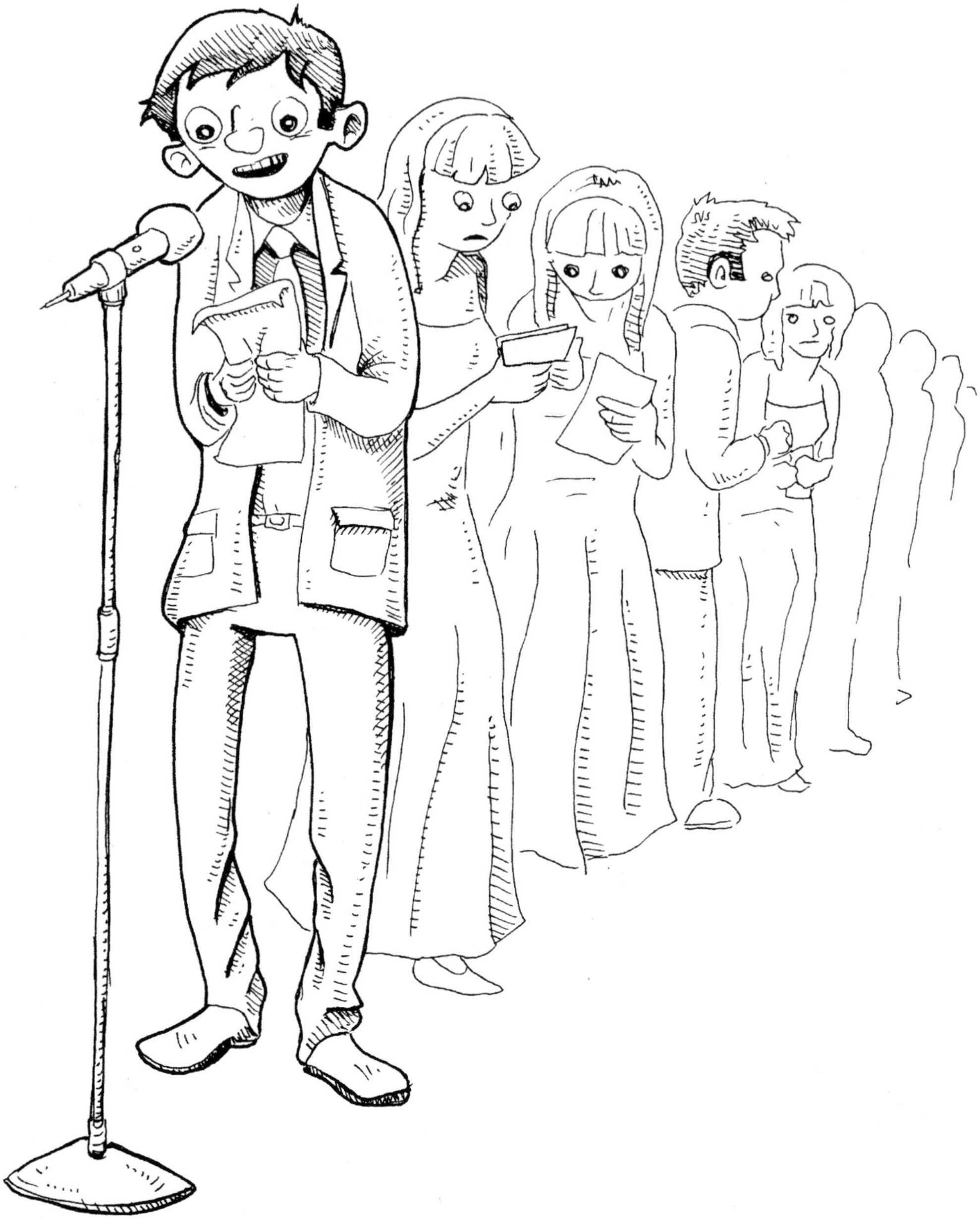

68

DON'T have more than three toasts

Usually one toast is enough to make people want to go to the coat check—mainly because most people just aren't creative and their toasts are absolutely terrible. It's always the same old boring crap: "Sandy and I met in college in our dorm room. Boy, we sure did have some good times." No one ever tells a great story. We shouldn't be telling you this, but your "toasters" need to make it personal—use visuals, be funny, and get the crowd into it. Who are we kidding? That's not going to happen—so, three boring toasts, no longer than three minutes each, is plenty of toasting for any one occasion. And make sure to thank your best man or maid of honor for working so hard on their toasts—we are sure that will really add to the night.

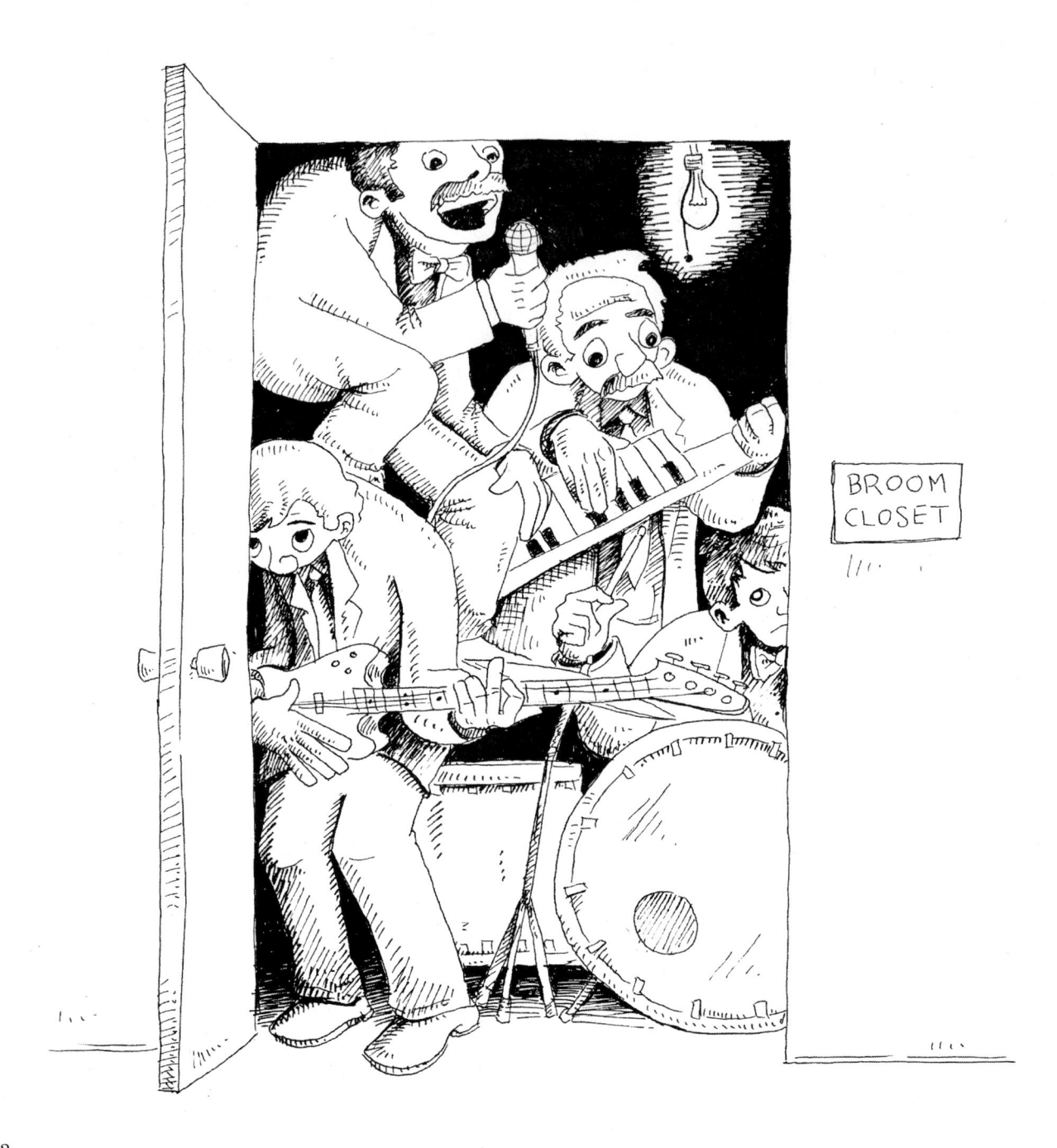

BROOM CLOSET

69

DON'T have a band in a small reception hall

Have you ever heard the phrase "fat guy in a little coat"? A good phrase—yes. A bad visual—also yes. This phrase, however, pretty much works for anything that is about to explode. Like your head after you get done writing thank-you notes for all the useless overpriced china gravy boats and butter dishes you just got. Which, by the way, you will only use once every four years when it's your turn to host Thanksgiving. It's also like at your reception if you have an eight-member band playing in a room the size of a broom closet. If you want a band, then you better get a big room or else plan on dealing with a bunch of old people suddenly becoming deaf. Hey, that might not be so bad—keep the small room.

144

70

DON'T crowd the dinner table with useless china

Most people do not need four spoons, three knives, and nine forks to eat. Nor do they need seven different sizes of plates and three glasses. Save the space on the already crowded table and limit the china to a reasonable amount. We can all do without the little mystery fork that everyone is unsure about until the know-it-all at the table pretends to actually know it all.

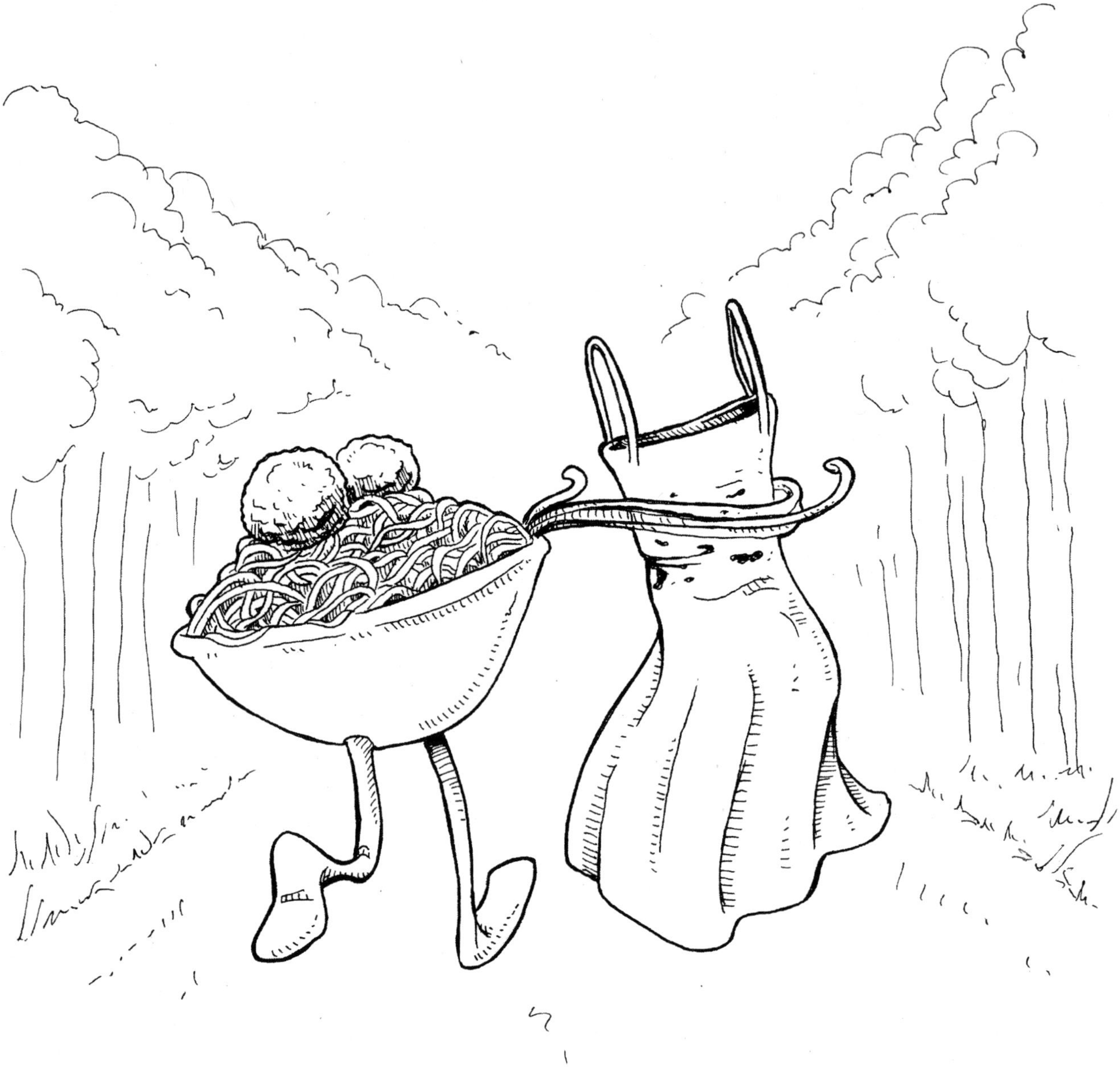

71

DON'T serve spaghetti

You might think that Mr. Spaghetti and Miss Formal Clothing hate each other. But in all actuality, they love each other. This is why Mr. Spaghetti is always trying to attach himself to Miss Formal Clothing. But, you certainly do not need to foster this relationship at your wedding reception. Keep Mr. Spaghetti away from the dinner table and keep Miss Formal Clothing looking her best.

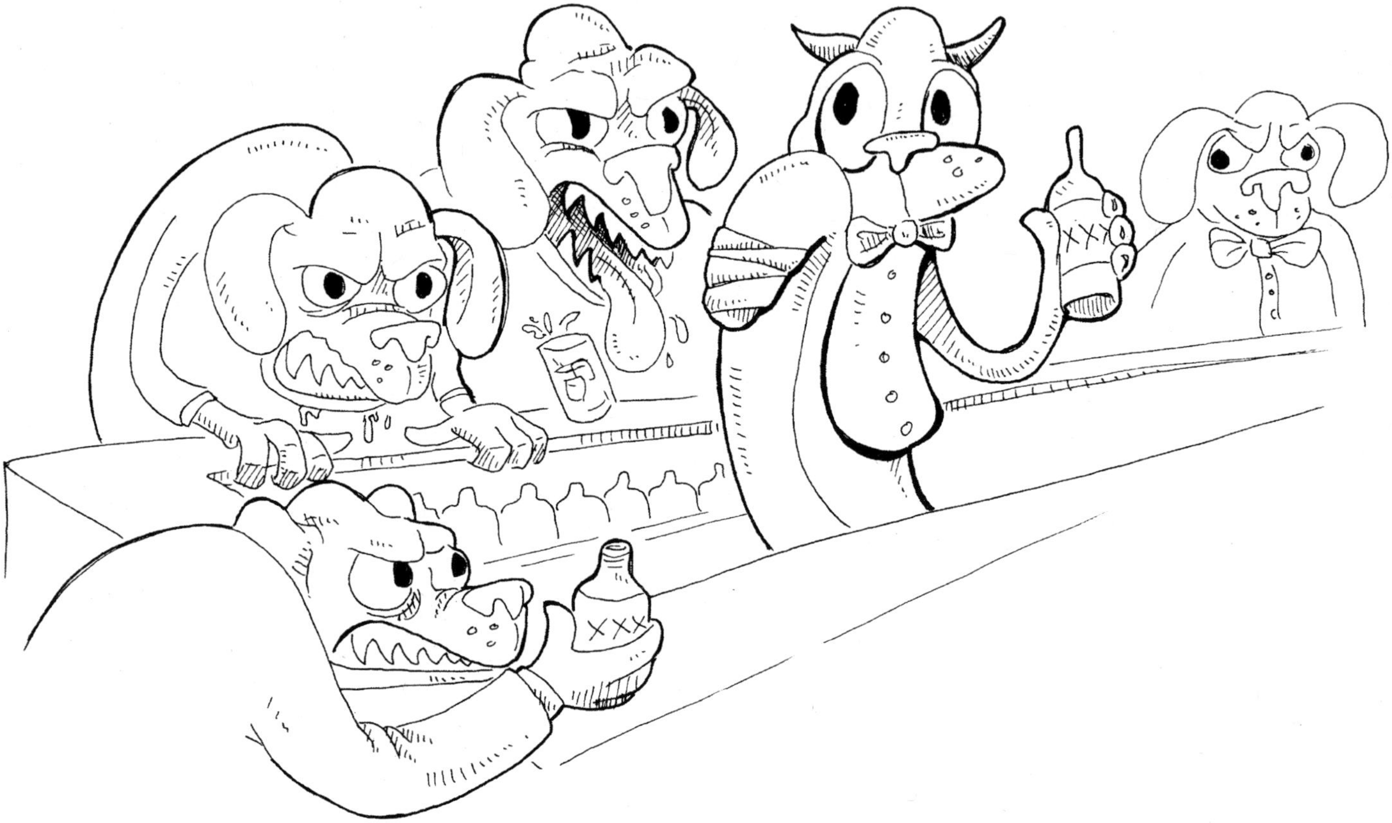

72

DON'T have 1 bartender for 200 people

Have you ever seen a pack of dogs attack a three-legged cat? If not, we are confident you can paint this picture in your head. Got the picture painted? Good, because this is what it will be like if you have a lack of bartenders for your rowdy group. A perfect ratio is one bartender for each and every person, but since that is just not economical these days, we recommend you stick with a ratio of one bartender per seventy-five people. And once you hit the 200 mark, you should probably add in an additional bar. Don't forget. Keep all bars close to the dance floor to ensure the maximum amount of not so sober dancing.

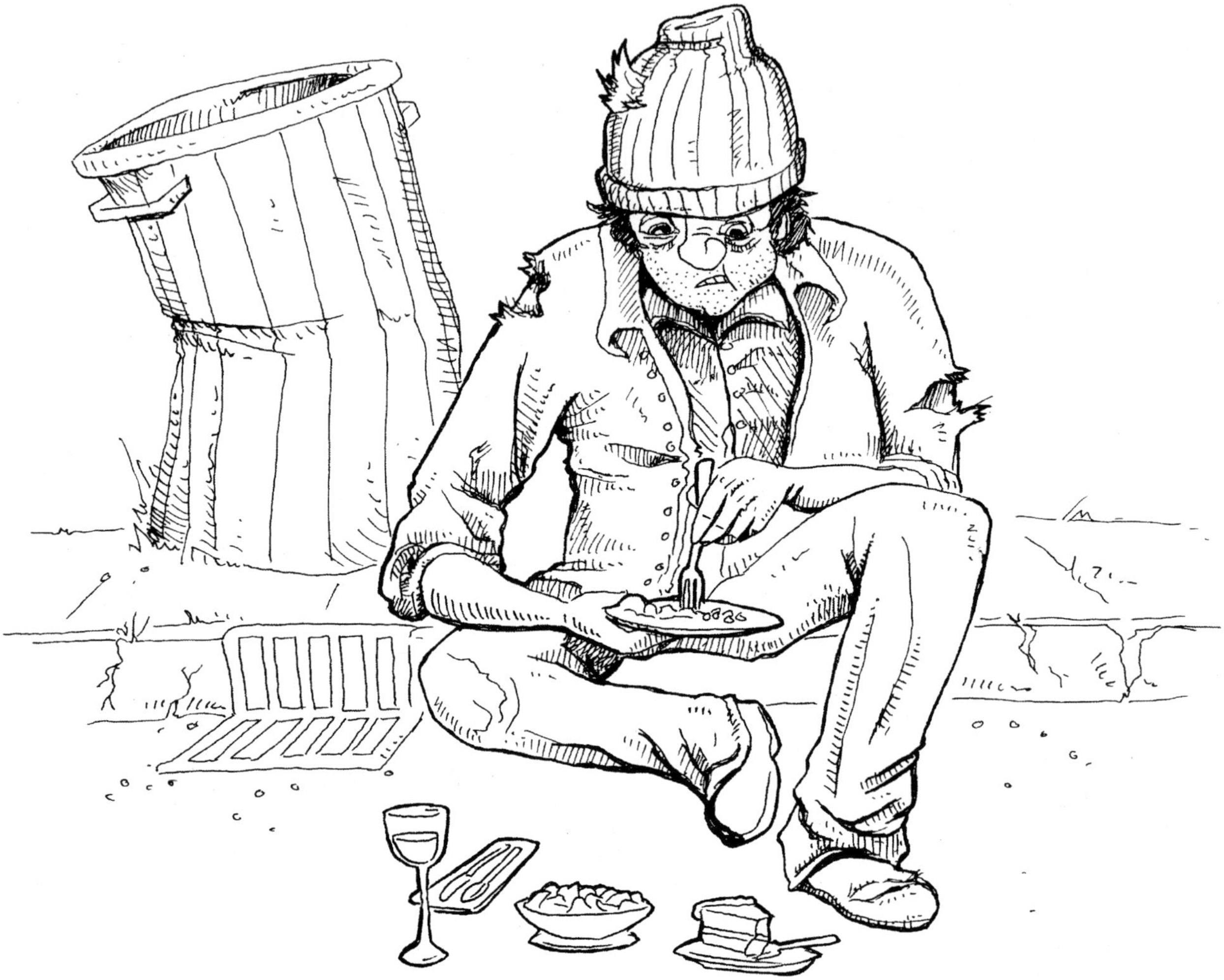

~ 73 ~

DON'T allow your caterer to serve less than you paid for

So you paid for 300 people, but only 270 showed up? Well, then the caterer should have thirty meals that you paid $50 each for ready for you to take home. Of course, you do not need thirty meals, but family and friends can take them for leftovers. Do you think you are going to get the $1,500 back from the caterer for those thirty meals? Absolutely not. At the very least have the food delivered to the local homeless. Certainly there are a few in your town in need of a sobering meal.

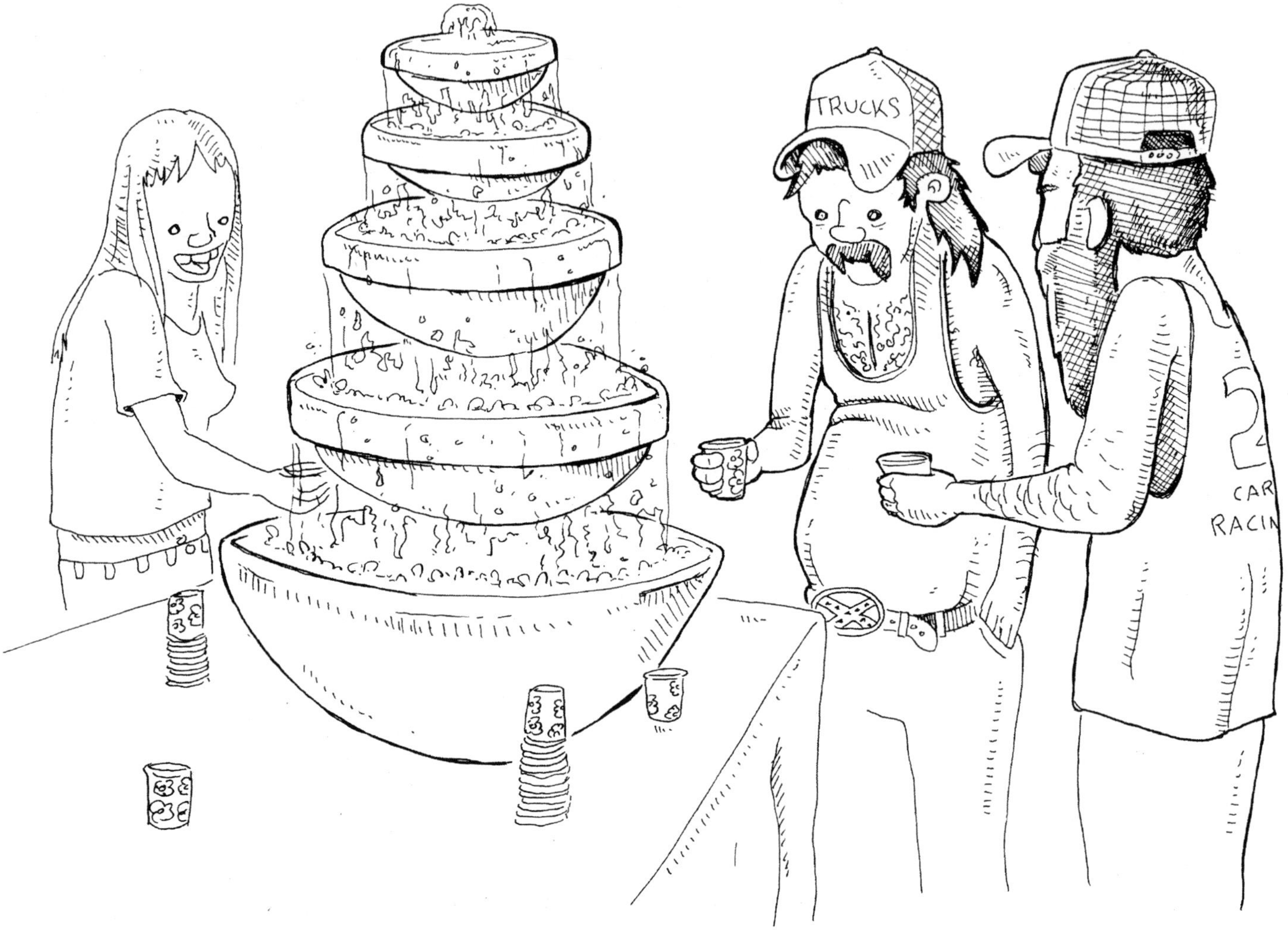
TRUCKS
2
CAR
RACIN

74

DON'T have a Boones Farm fountain

Oh yeah—we have seen it. While it did taste delicious and did attract quite a crowd, a Boones Farm fountain will add a certain "feeling" that we are not so sure you are going for at your wedding. One exception does apply: If you are having your wedding at the VFW hall and the father of the bride is wearing a tuxedo-print T-shirt, then a Boones Farm fountain actually becomes a luxury item and is very acceptable. Otherwise, we suggest you save your guests the stomachache and stick with cheap wine from a box. Hey, we never said anything about saving your guests from a headache.

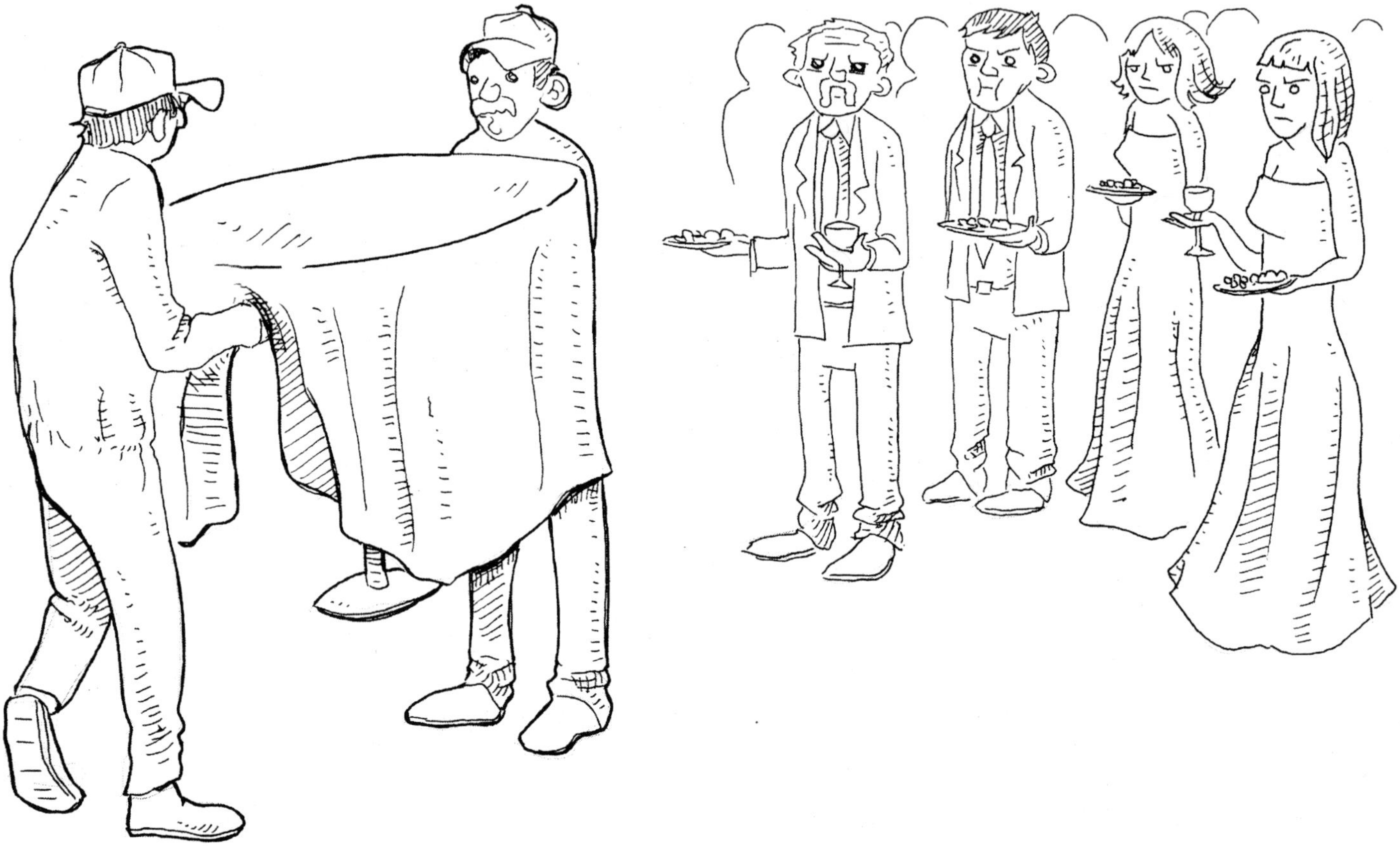

75

DON'T put tables on the dance floor

What happens to the people who lose their tables once dancing starts? Well, they usually just leave because they now have nowhere to sit. Keep your dance floor clear all night. Guests might even like to do some slow dancing in between dinner courses.

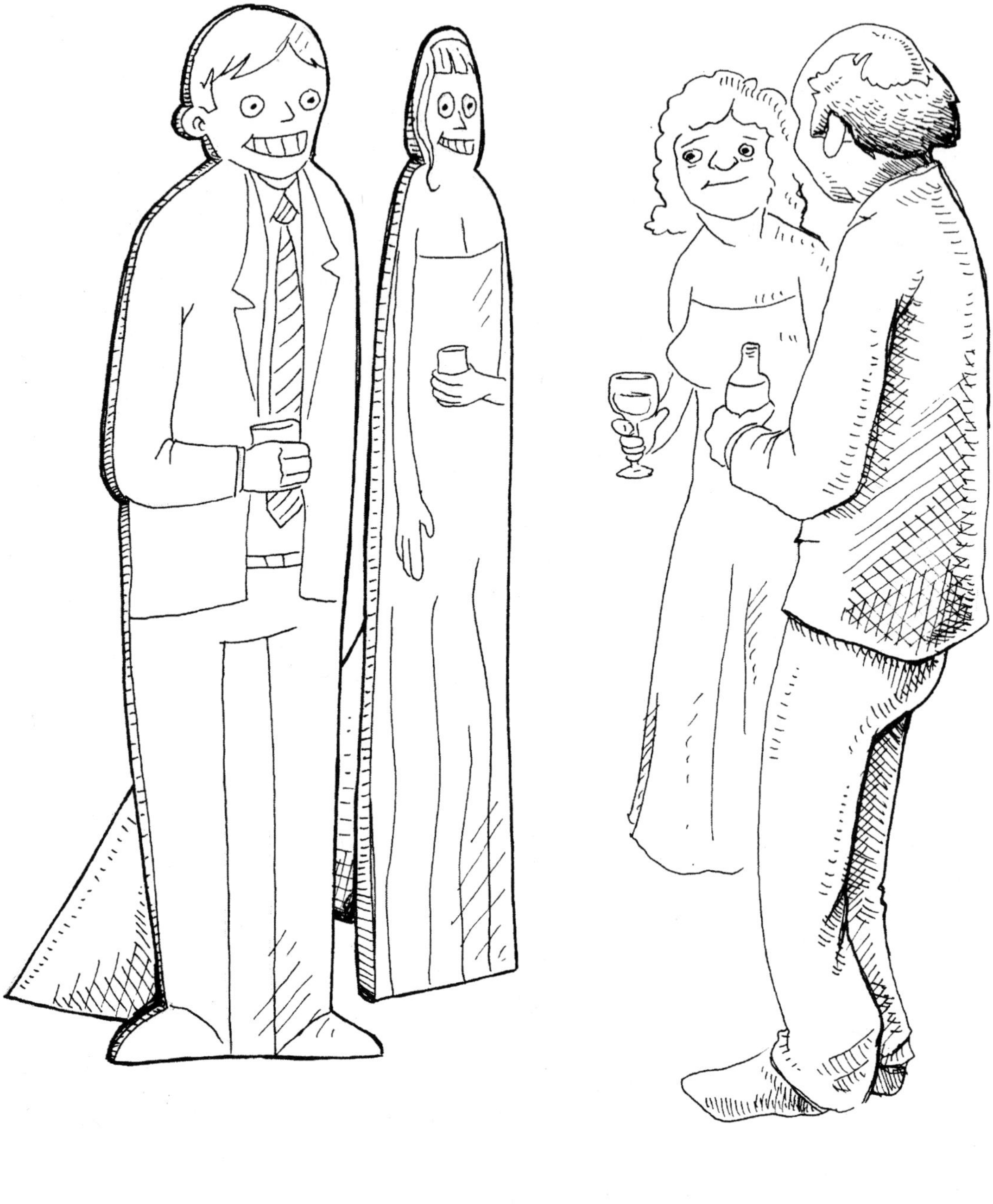

76

DON'T forget to enjoy your cocktail hour

Cocktail hour is an hour filled with cocktails—and conversation with your friends and family. Don't miss out on it because you are driving around in a limo or taking pictures out under a gazebo by a lake. Spend the time with the people who are there to see you.

158

77

DON'T have your wedding in an old mansion

Old mansions are dumb. Why? Well, because everything is old. Because the rooms are small, and the ceilings are low. Because the power is inadequate for your vendors. Because the A/C is about as reliable as a deadbeat dad. Because the bathrooms are tiny. Because the floors creak. Because the parking is a pain. Because the neighborhoods often have noise curfews at 10:00 PM. But mostly, however, old mansions are terrible because no matter where you go you know you might break something expensive at any time.

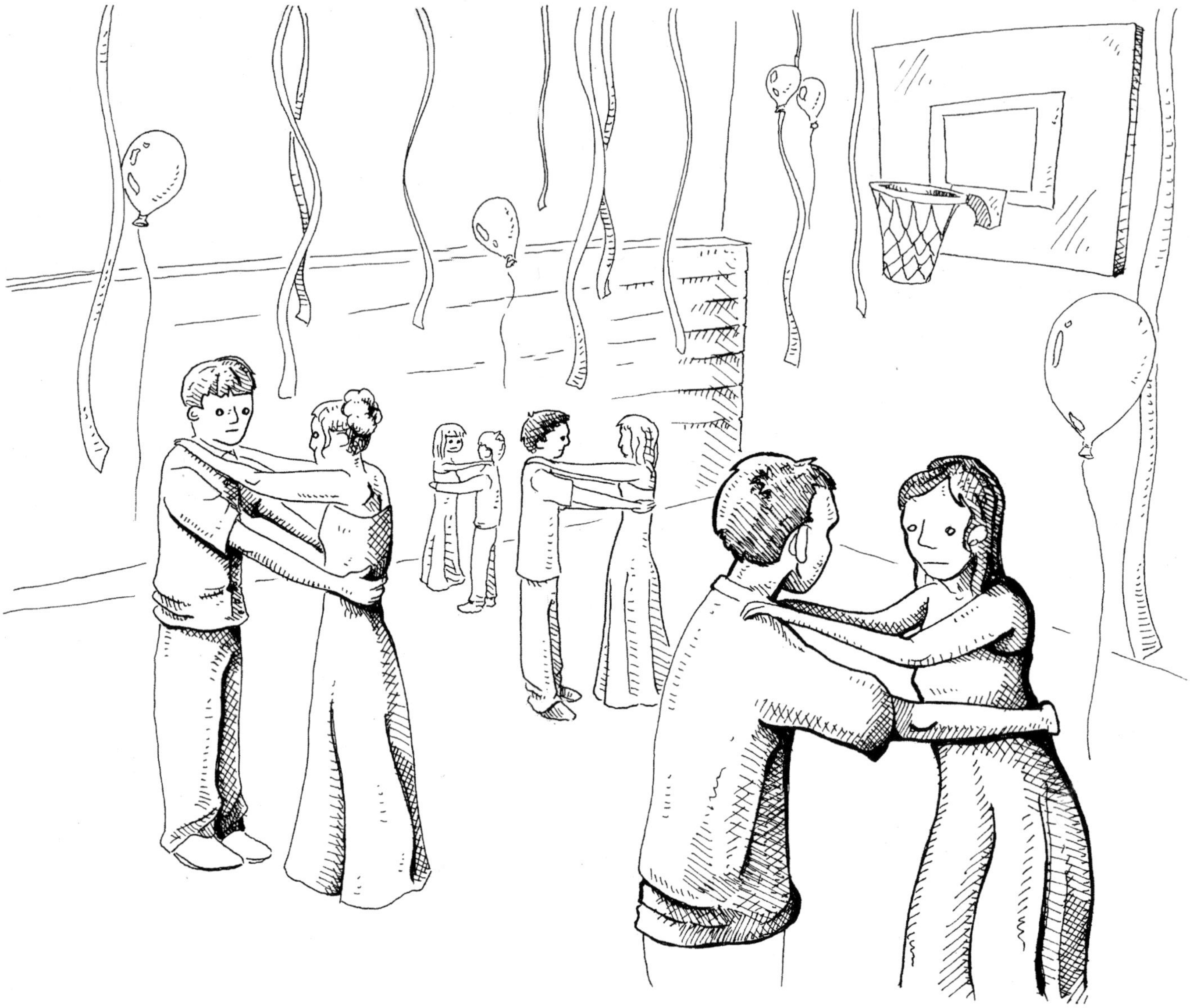

78

DON'T make your wedding party dance with each other

Watching the wedding party dance is about as comfortable as a church pew. It feels like the 8th grade dance all over again. If you must have a wedding party dance (see reason #25), then please at least allow your party the ability to dance with their own dates.

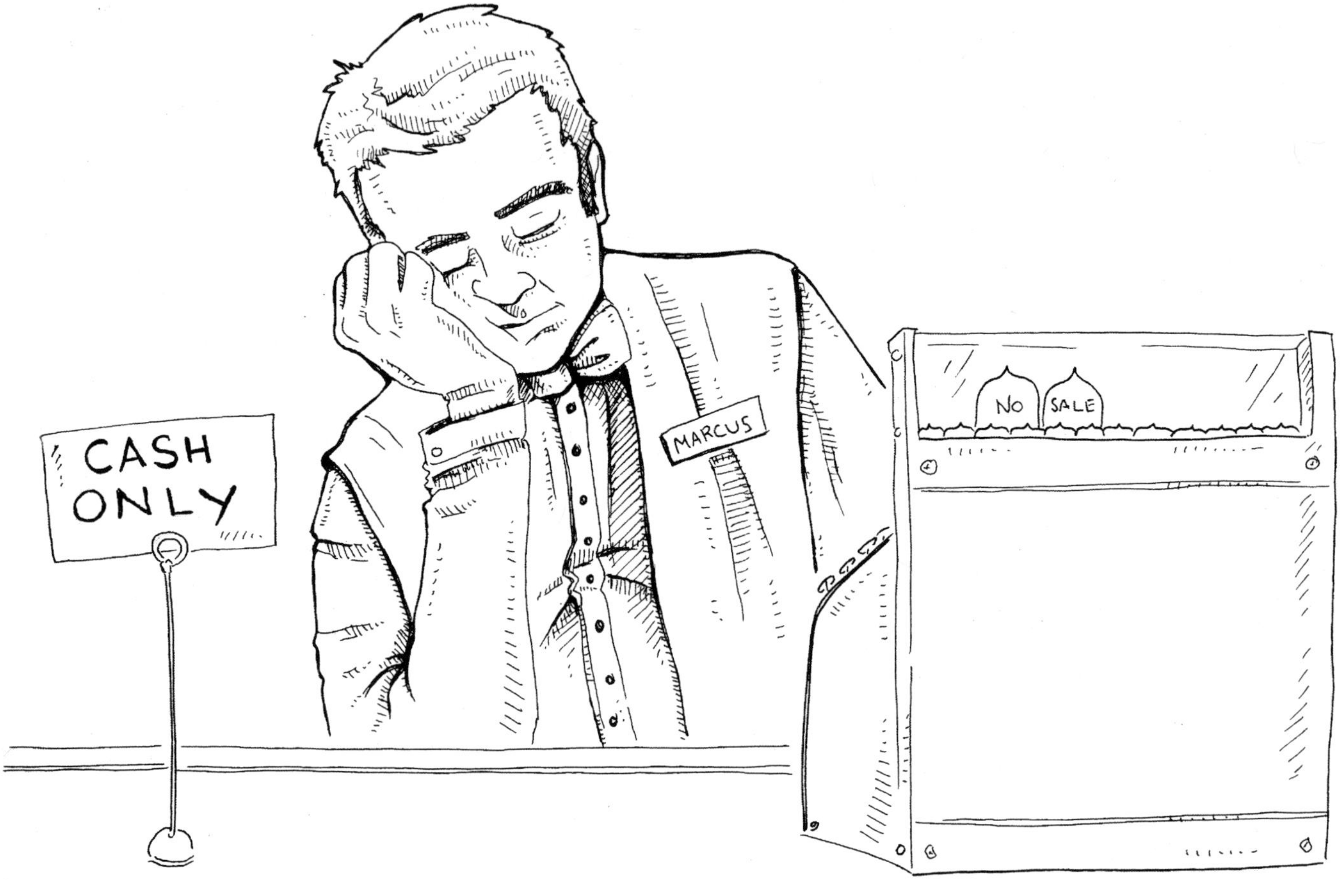
CASH ONLY
MARCUS
NO
SALE

79

DON'T have a cash bar

If you are actually considering a cash bar, then you should actually consider not having a reception.

∞ 80 ∞

DON'T force your friends to spend a fortune to be in your wedding party

Wedding costs are like Greg's sister Lindsey at her 21st birthday party—totally out of control. And while you may have money saved up, your wedding party probably does not have an endless stream of cash to fund the clothing requirements you are imposing on them. One hundred dollars seems fair to ask a friend to spend on clothing for your wedding. Anything more and you should offer to help out with the costs.

OUR LOVE POEM
OUR LOVE POEM
OUR LOVE POEM
OUR LOVE POEM
OUR LOVE POEM

81

DON'T give stupid souvenirs to your guests

No need to spend a ton of time packing up little chocolates in mesh bags with special passages attached. Most of these end up on the tables or in the trash can at the end of the night. People don't actually get excited to eat the chocolate—nor do they get energized to read the passage.

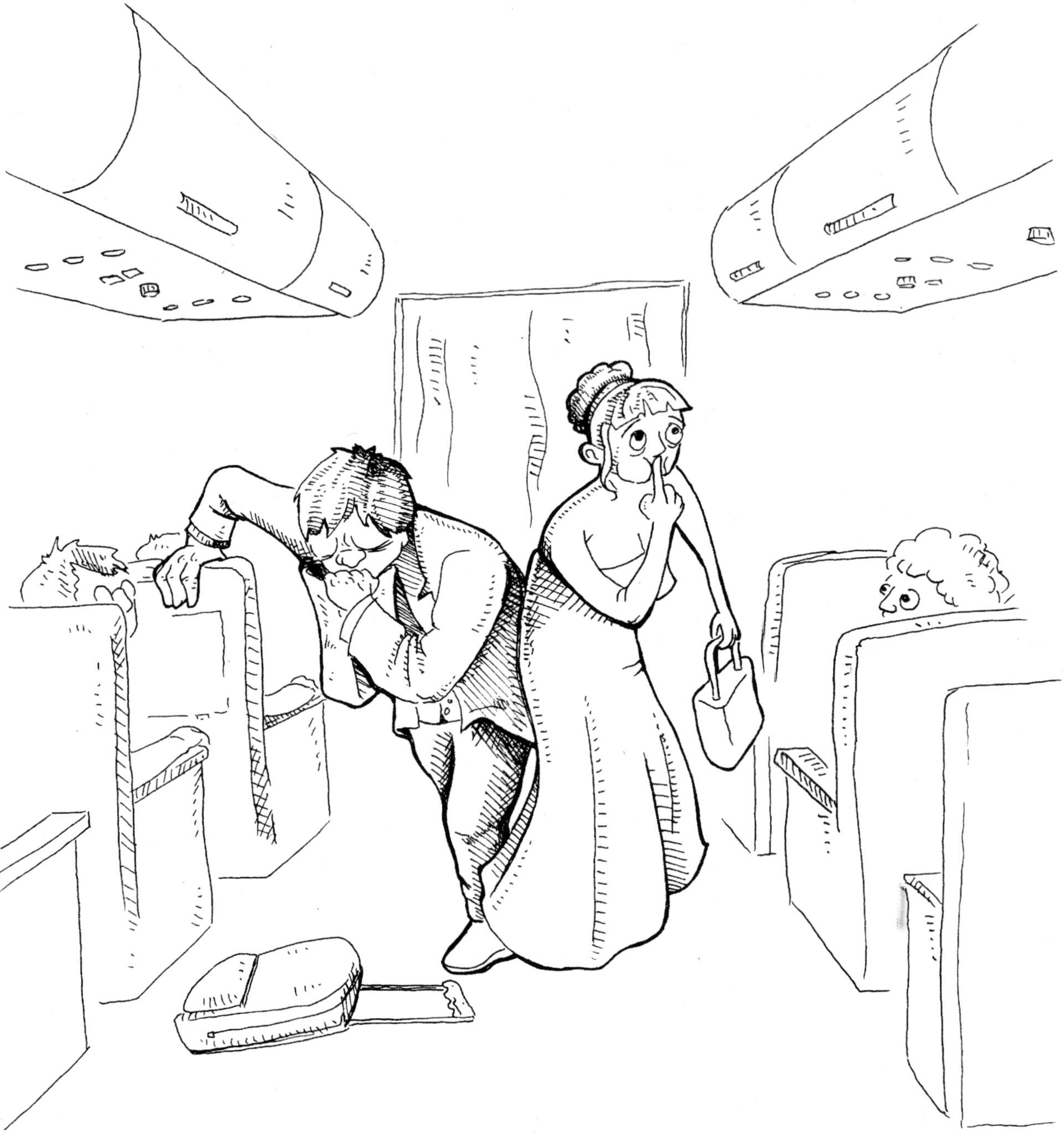

82

DON'T leave for your honeymoon at 7:00 AM the next morning

After your wedding, you will be very tired. You will also have a very bad headache. Hopping on a plane in the morning and traveling all day is going to sound about as exciting as another Jaeger bomb. Spend the Sunday with your close family and friends who are still in town. Relax and leave on Monday.

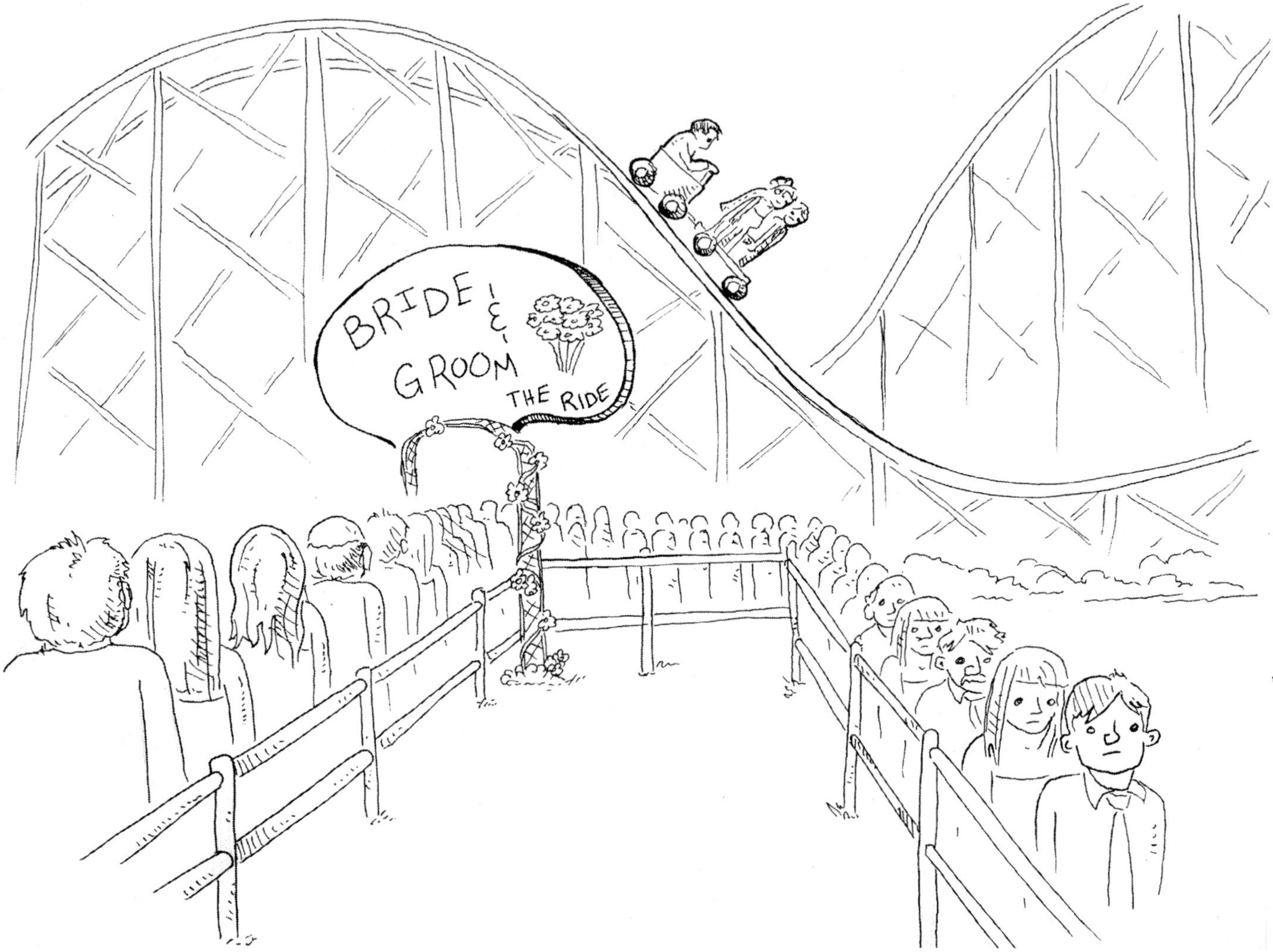
BRIDE & GROOM
THE RIDE

83

DON'T have a receiving line

Yeah, yeah, yeah, we all know that your guests are happy to see you. But your wedding is not an amusement park, and you are not a ride. So don't make them wait in a long line for a five-second, "Hi, congratulations, we are so happy for you." There will be plenty of time for that during the reception.

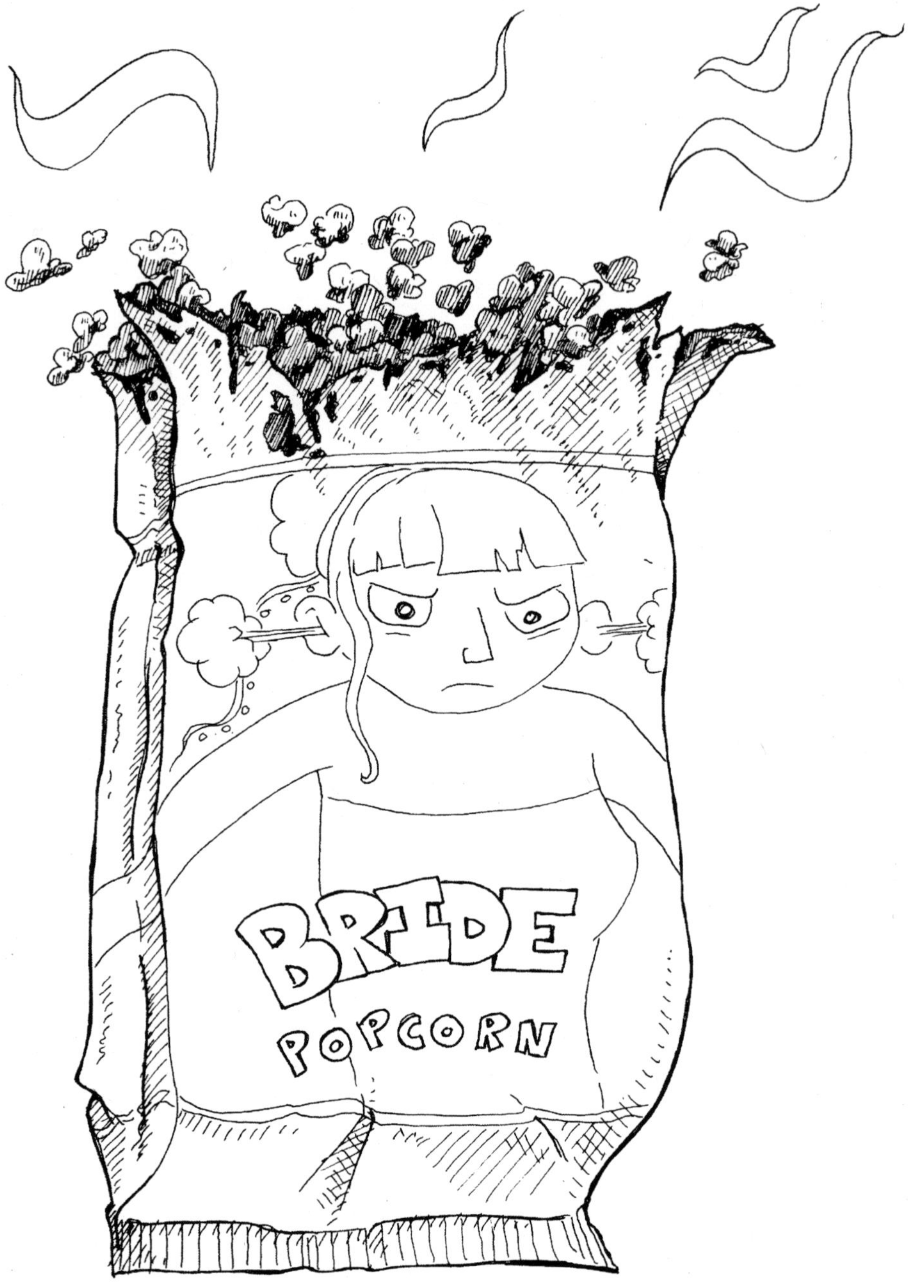
BRIDE
POPCORN

84

DON'T make the bride aware of wedding day problems

A bride on her wedding day is like a bag of unpopped popcorn. The more heat, or "problems," you tell her about during the day, the hotter she will get. Eventually her kernels will start to pop and then burn—and once this happens, the rest of the day will just stink.

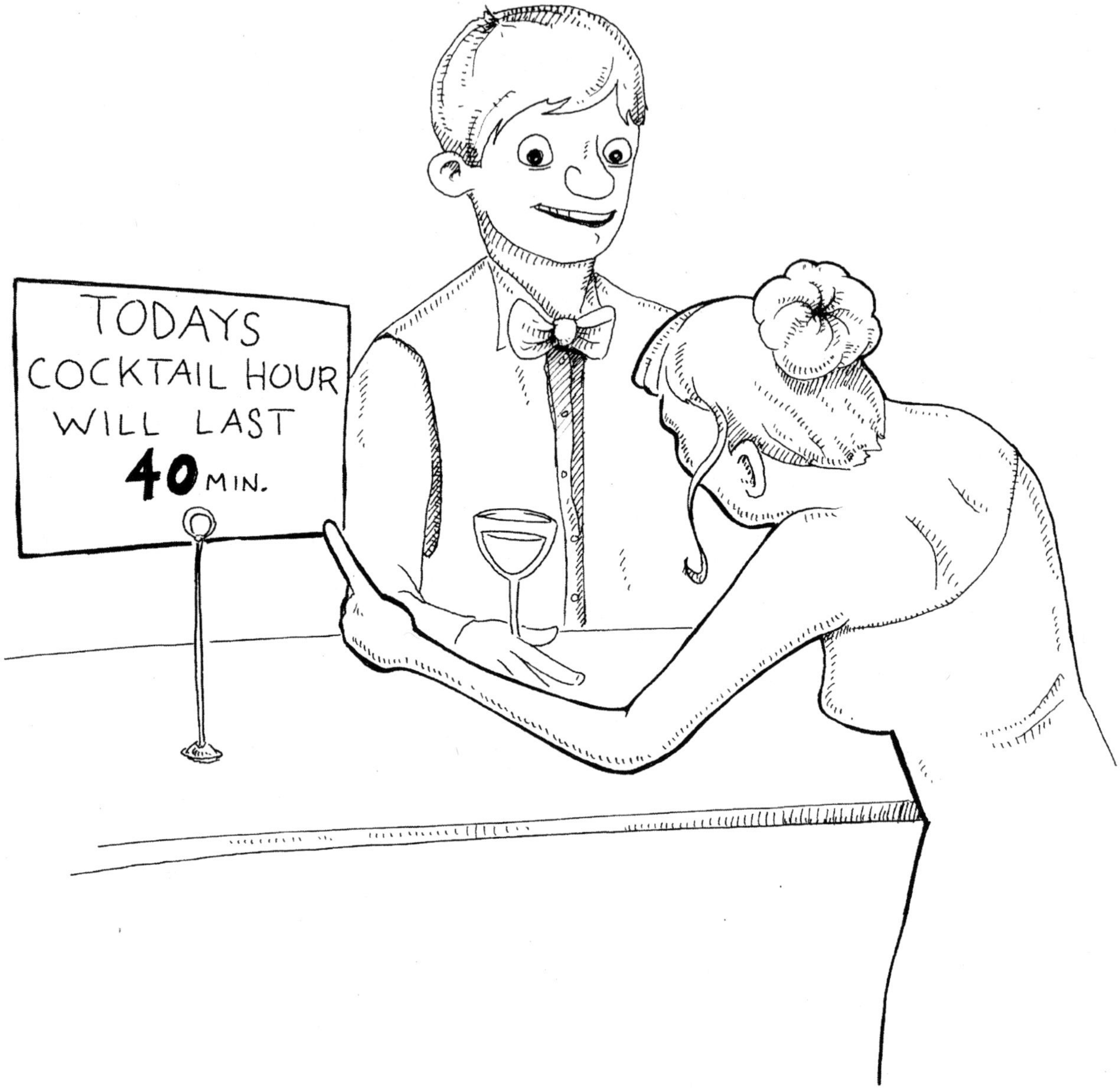
TODAYS
COCKTAIL HOUR
WILL LAST
40 MIN.

85

DON'T have a cocktail hour that lasts less than an hour

The bottom line here is that the phrase "cocktail hour" includes an important time indicator, the word "hour." An hour equals 60 minutes, or 3,600 seconds. In order to stay on the tight dinner schedule, many banquet coordinators try and start to move people during cocktail hour at the 40-minute mark to get everyone seated for dinner so they can keep the night moving. So, in conclusion, your guests miss out on a true cocktail hour, and you miss out on twenty minutes of booze that you paid for. Depending on who you invite to your wedding, it could be a lot of booze.

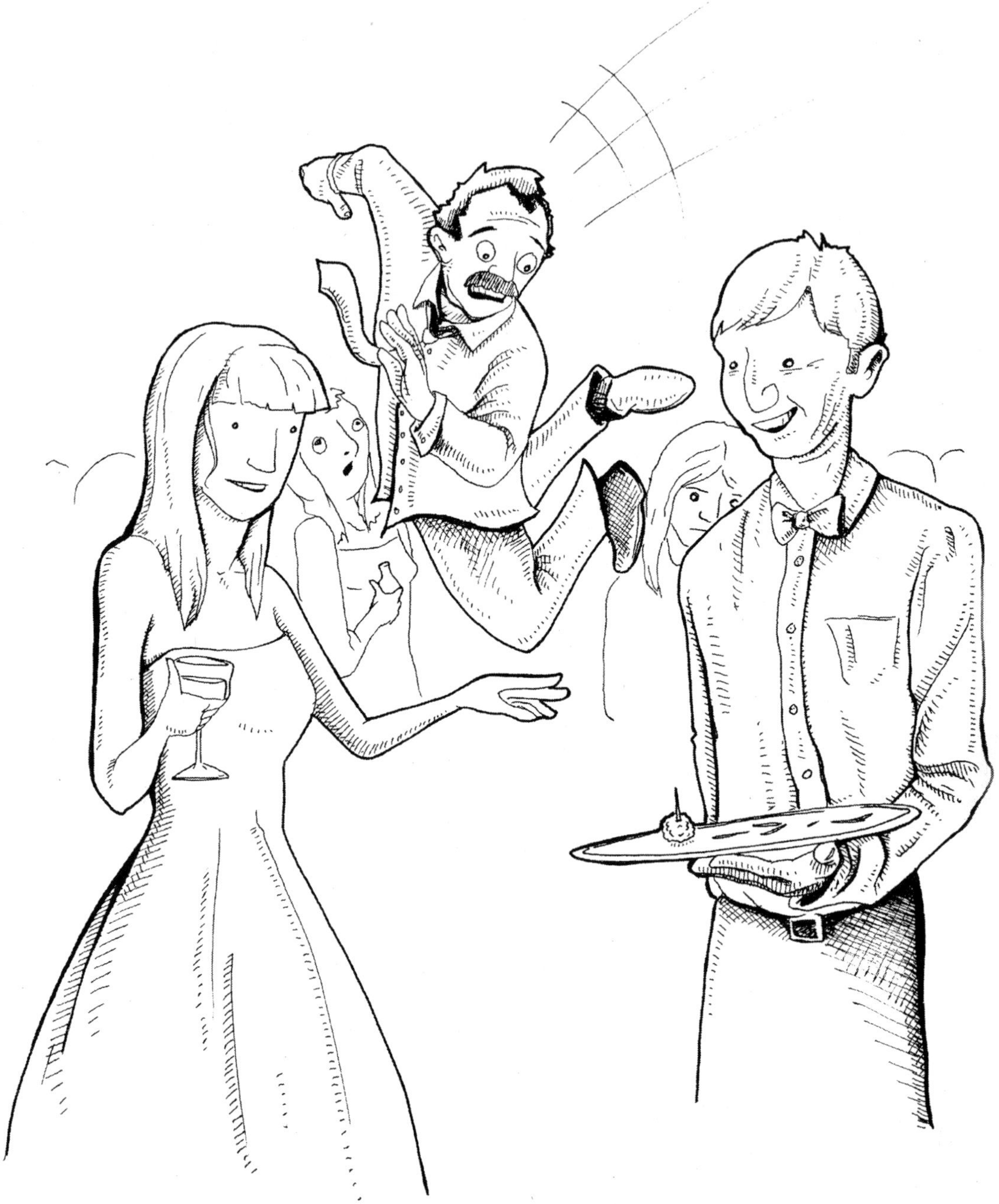

86

DON'T serve hors d'oeuvres unless you have enough for everyone

You spot it—across the room—a woman in black pants and white blouse. It looks like she is carrying—yes, she has the delicious meatball platter and is headed your way. Here she comes—almost there. Hey, wait a minute. The tray is looking low—way too low. Damn, that guy just grabbed the last meatball. You think to yourself: "I wonder when the waiter will be back with another round?" The answer: Never.

Hors d'oeuvres never seem to even make it around the room once. Why? Because caterers are cheap. Make sure there is enough for everyone—or don't offer them at all.

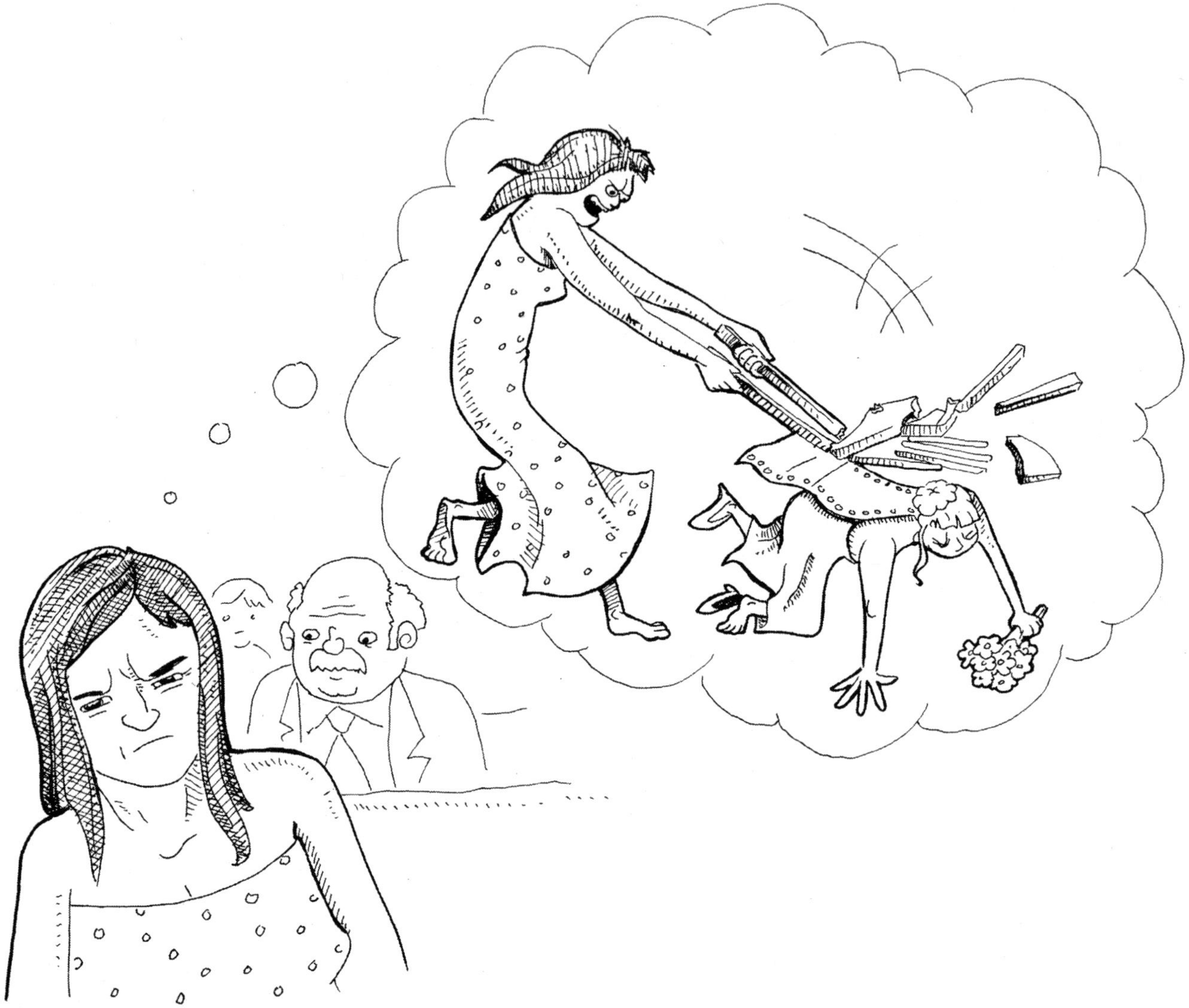

87

DON'T invite your ex's to the wedding

A man and a woman will never be totally 100 percent "just friends." There is always some point in the relationship, even after a breakup, where one thinks of the other in a romantic way and asks themselves "what if?" Now, do you want your future spouse's ex at your wedding wondering "what if?" We think "no" is probably the right answer here. Take a listen to Garth Brooks' "Friends in Low Places" if you need additional information.

88

DON'T introduce everyone in the grand entrance

If you introduce everyone, then who will be there to witness the grand entrance? Seriously, your entire extended family and network of friends do not need to be formally introduced to the entire room. Why? Well, because nobody cares. Keep it simple and small—your wedding party and your parents should do it.

DIRECTIONS

- LEFT
- LEFT
- RIGHT
- LEFT
- GO STRAIGHT
- RIGHT
- LEFT
- ARRIVE

89

DON'T provide half ass driving directions

Pull out of the church and take a right. Then go down the road and make a left after the big tree. Go past the blue windmill and then turn right at the farm. The reception hall is down the road just past the flagpole.

Let's be honest with ourselves here folks. These kinds of directions, while commonplace, are about as helpful as the average employee at the Department of Motor Vehicles. It's time to get specific with road names and distances. Don't assume your guests have common sense. In fact, don't assume anyone has common sense.

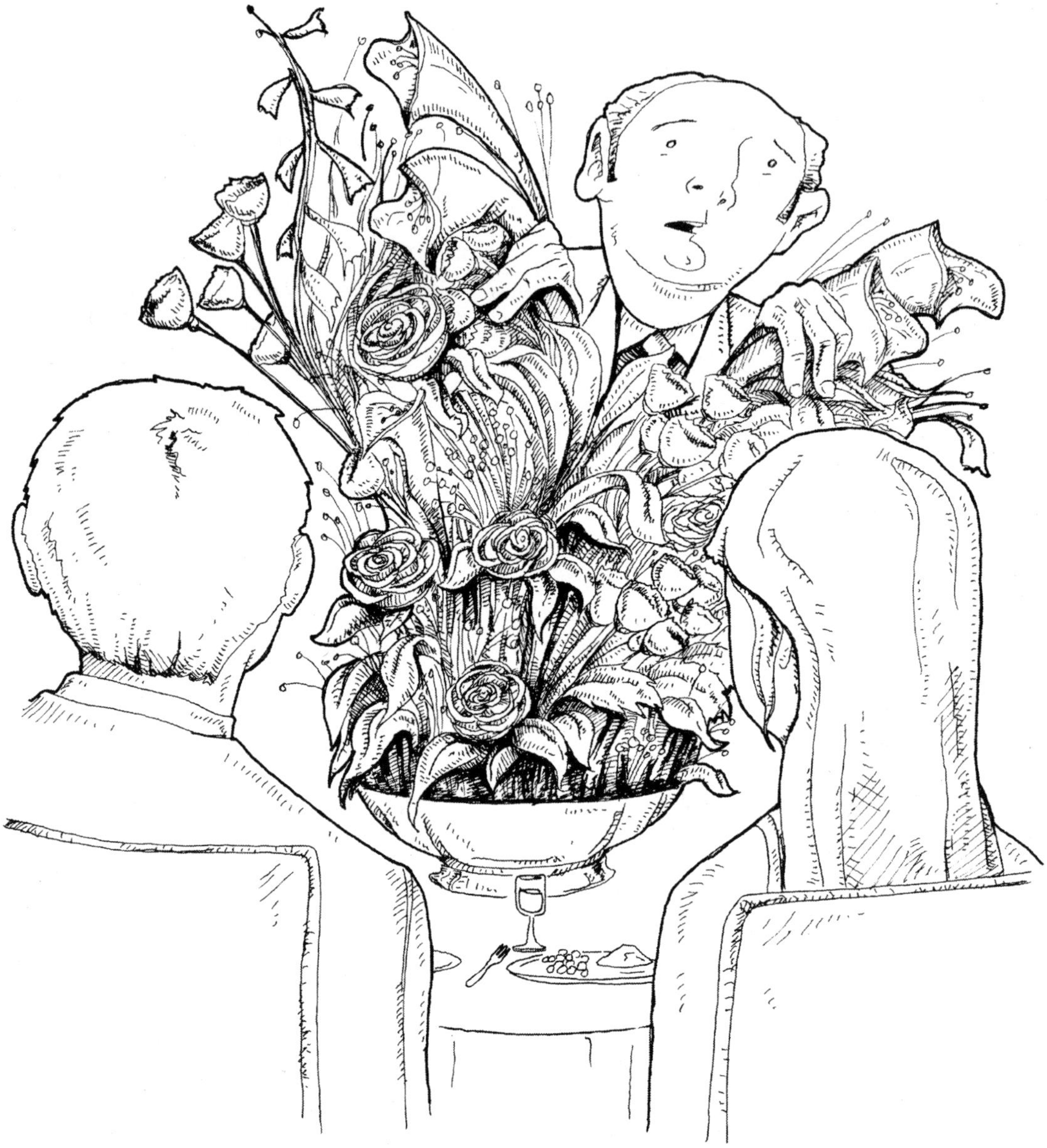

90

DON'T have huge flower arrangements on the tables

How in the world do you expect your friend Cyndee to meet your cousin Jason or your boss Matthew to sit and chat with your brother-in-law Tommy with a gigantic tree in the middle of the table? We are not at Yosemite here. Get rid of the huge unnecessarily expensive flower arrangement and keep it simple—no need to make your guests feel like they are spying on the person across the table through a massive amount of foliage.

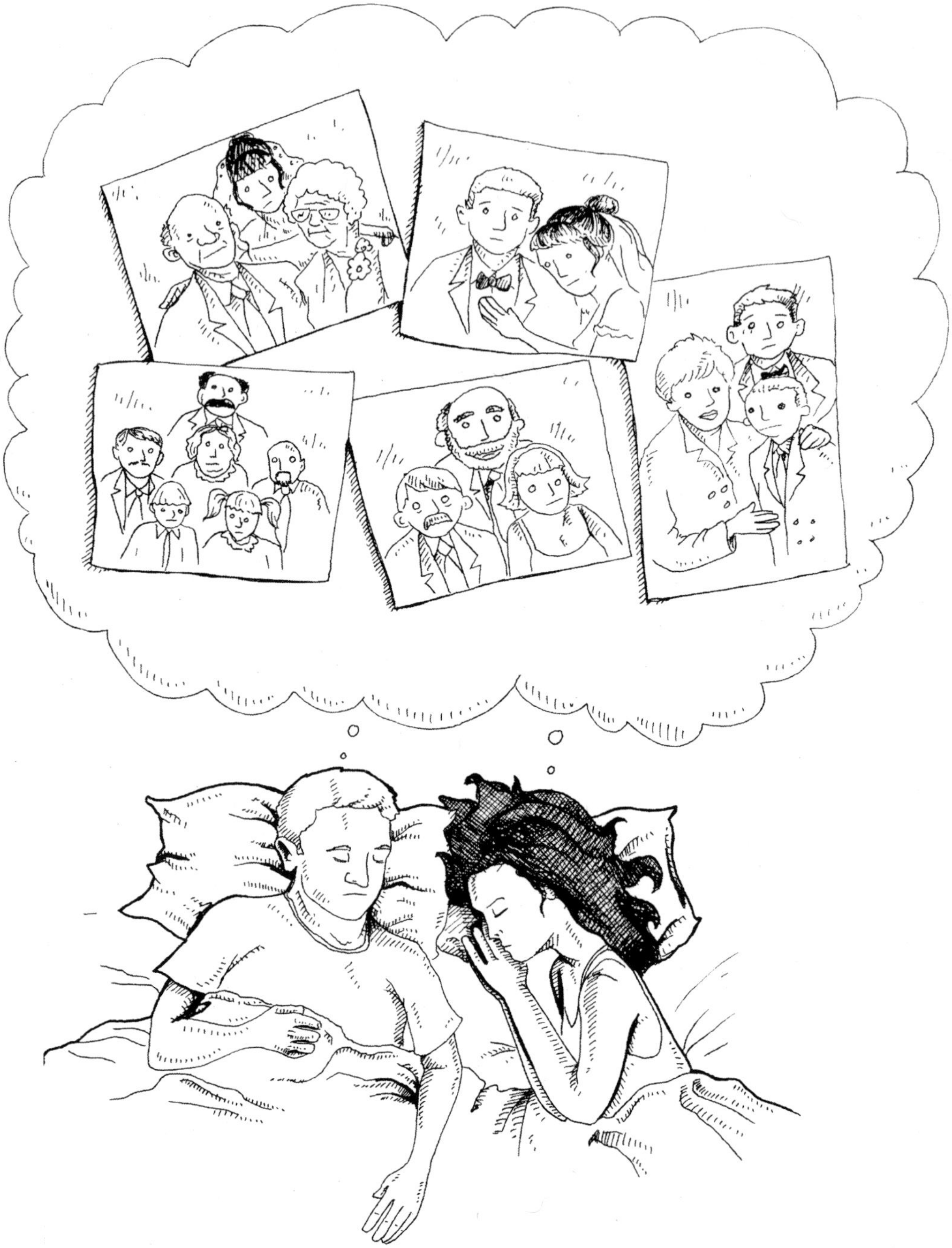

91

DON'T spend your entire reception taking pictures in the hallway

We know pictures are important—and you definitely want to have some great ones. You did hire a professional photographer after all. But, do not forget to enjoy the wedding, your family and friends, and the party. We have been to so many weddings where the photographer has the bride and groom out taking pictures all night with every family combination known to man. So what do you end up with at the end of your wedding night? A ton of family pictures. And a ton of memories about taking family pictures.

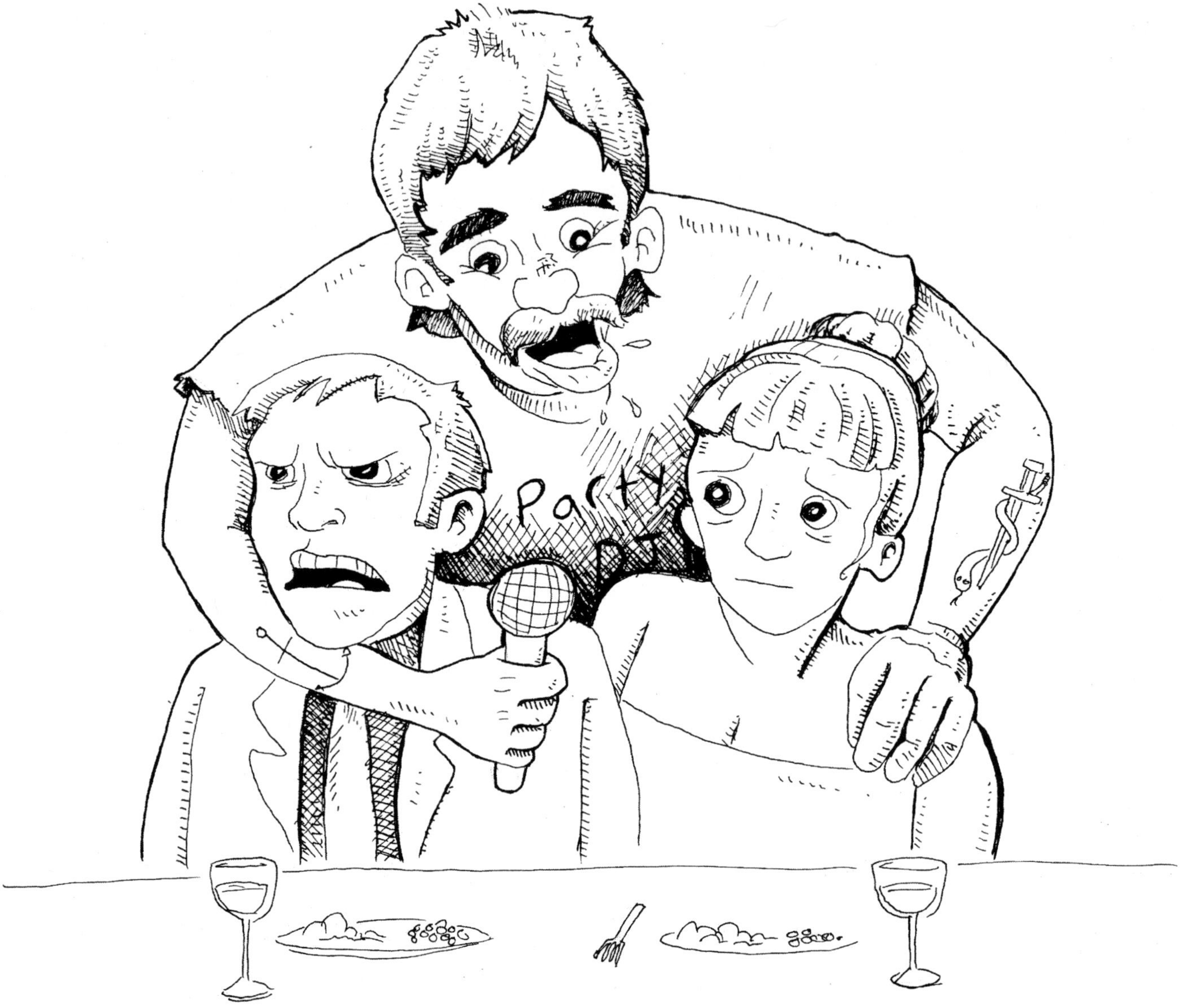
Party

92

DON'T let your DJ give a toast

You cannot make these up, folks. We never did this of course, but we have attended weddings where DJs have given toasts. And what horrible, uncomfortable, and impersonal moments they were.

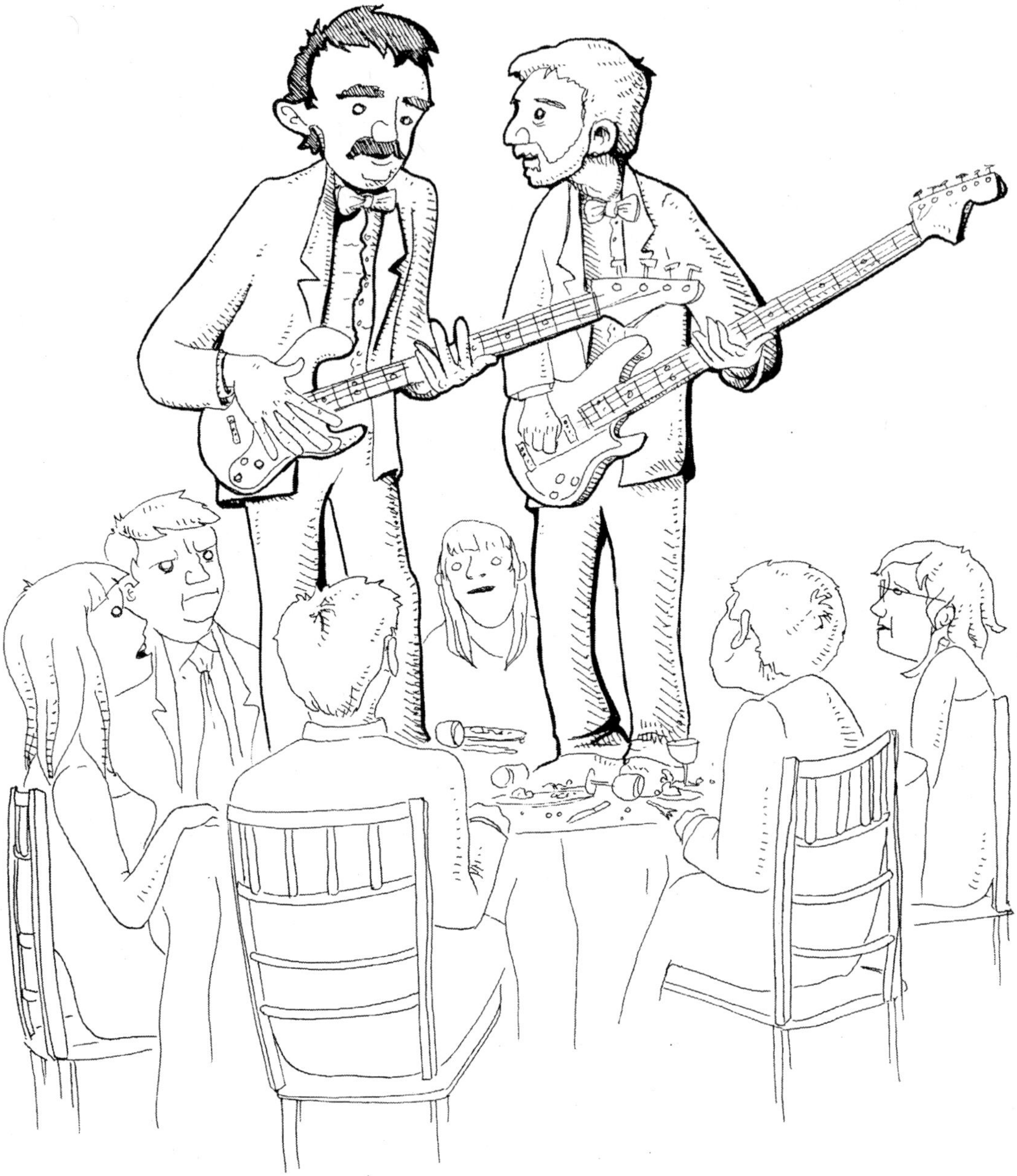

93

DON'T assume that the band will bring everything

Do assume that the band will bring their instruments, amplifiers, speakers, ridiculous clothing, drugs, and alcohol. *Do not* assume that they will bring dance lights, staging, or a clear head. You will need the staging to get them off the ground, at least 18' high, 25' long, and 20' deep (but check with the band for exact requirements). You will also want some dance lighting to help create the party dancing mood. We are sorry to say but just being at your wedding will not always do the trick.

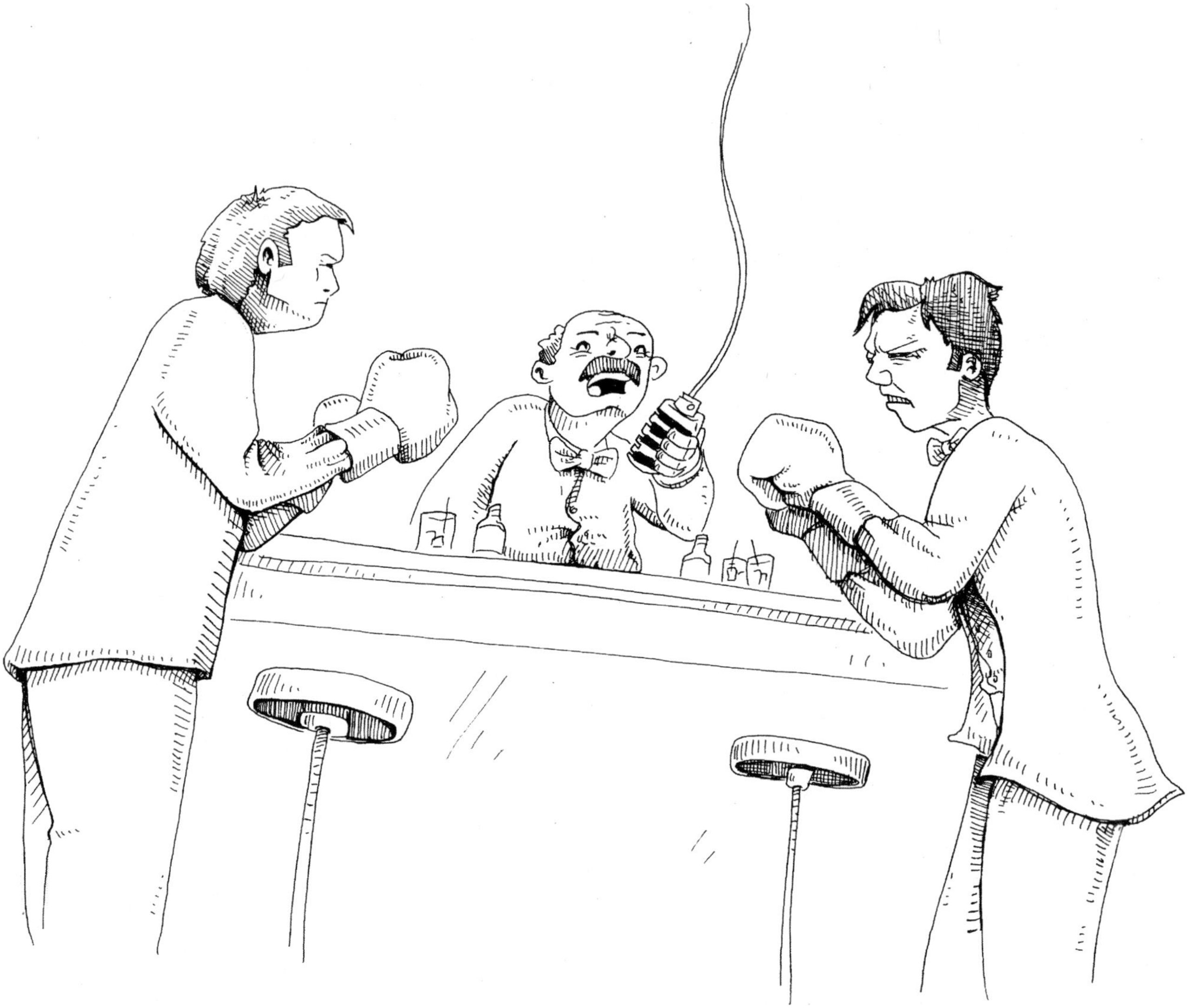

94

DON'T share a bar with another wedding

Sometimes guys like to fight for no reason when they get farther and farther away from soberness. Sharing a common bar can lead to territorial issues with these types of males. Thus, reinforcing their need to fight for no reason. If you foresee this as a problem, then steer clear from the shared bar—or get ready to share an ambulance.

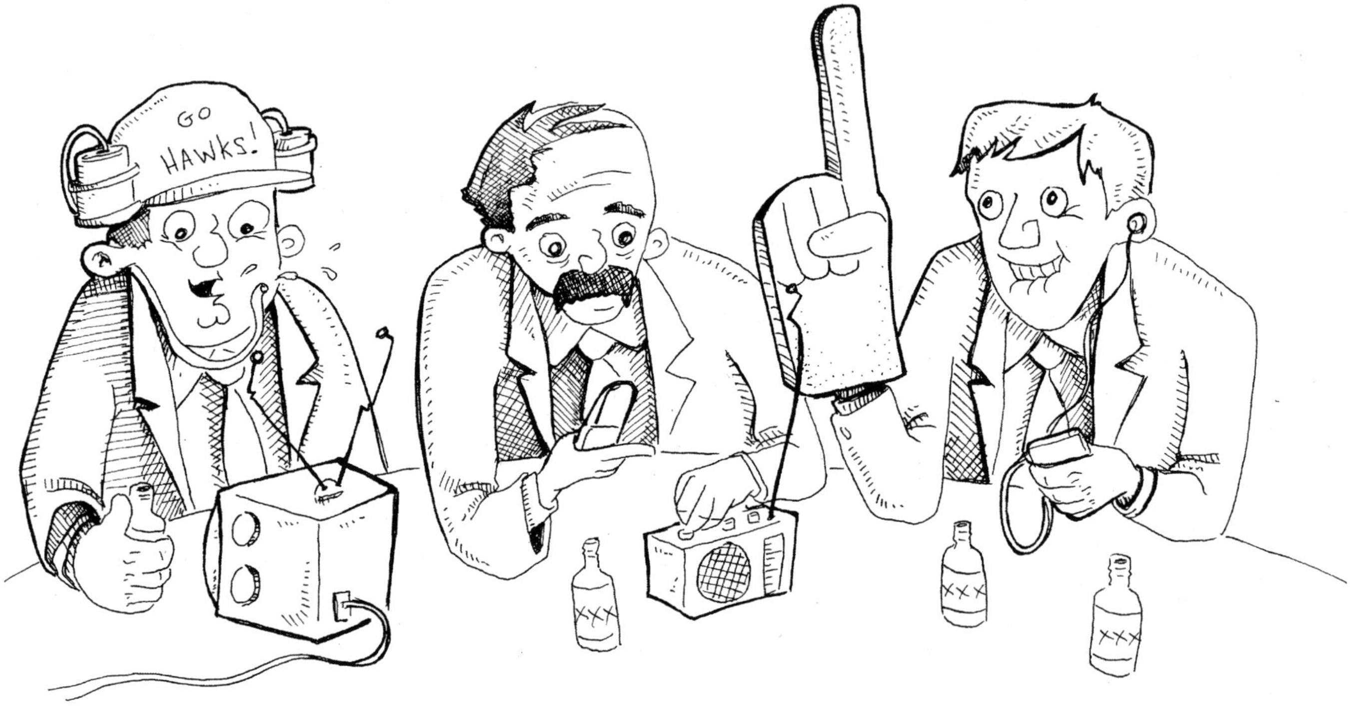
GO
HAWKS!

95

DON'T schedule your wedding during a major sporting event

To the average male, major sporting events are like women with large breasts walking down the street. They must not be missed. Even if that means being absent for a good portion of your wedding reception. Schedule your wedding during college bowl games, March Madness, the World Series, or any other major sporting event and you will be sorry. We have seen people listening to AM radios through earpieces, constantly checking their cell phones for score updates, and even huddled in a corner around a portable TV just to catch the action. Check the sports schedules and choose an alternate weekend—there are plenty more.

196

96

DON'T play music that your guests cannot dance to

It's awkward enough to have to watch your guests try to dance—
do 'em a favor and make sure the music is danceable.

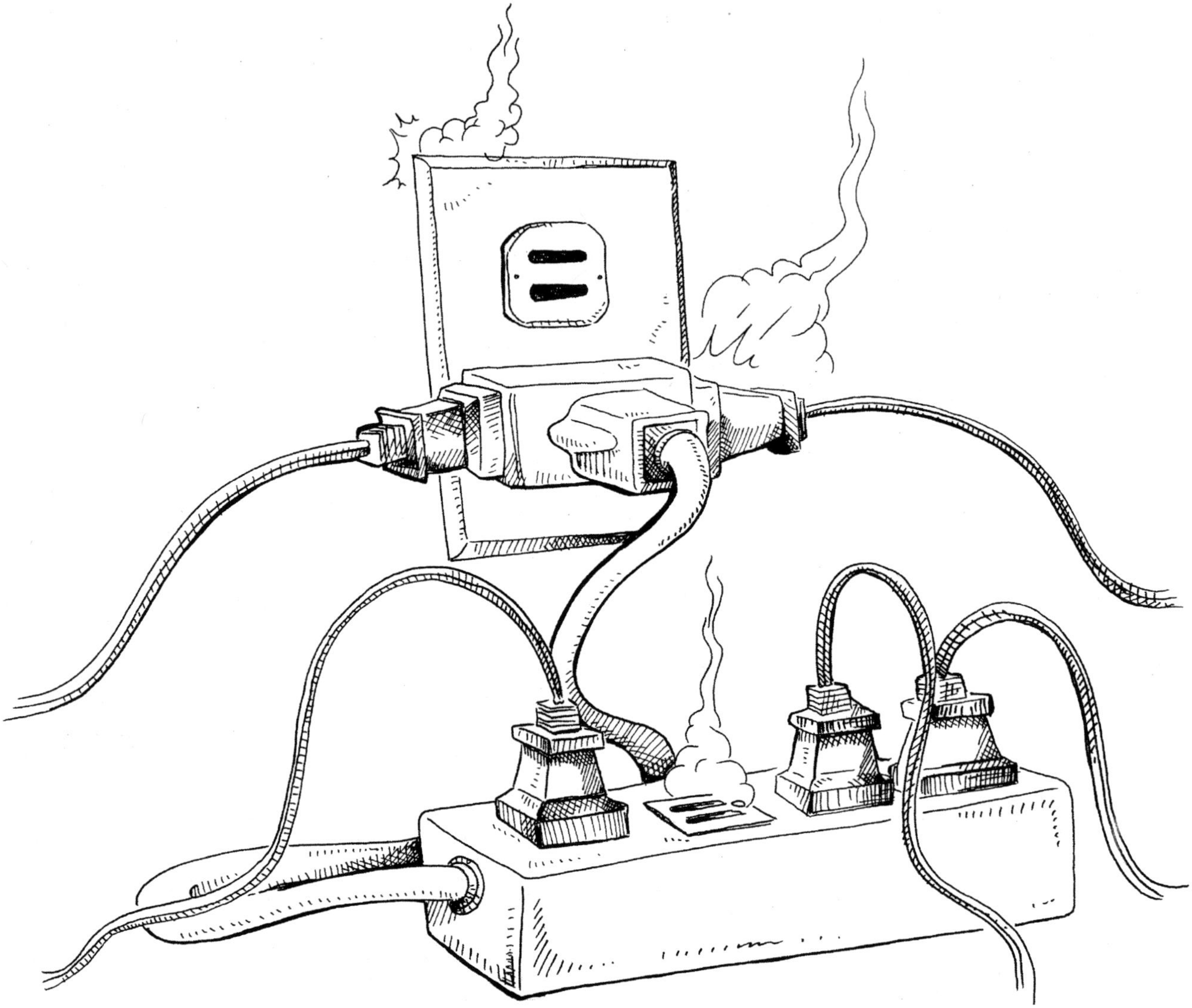

97

DON'T choose a location with substandard power

You might not think this is a problem, but it can be. If you select an older venue for your reception, then don't be surprised if your DJ's sound and lighting suddenly shuts down during the climax of "The Humpty Dance." In the wedding industry, this is what we call a "show stopper." Most DJs should require at least two 3-prong 120V, 20 amp outlets on two separate circuits, one for sound and one for lighting. Confirm this power availability before booking your venue.

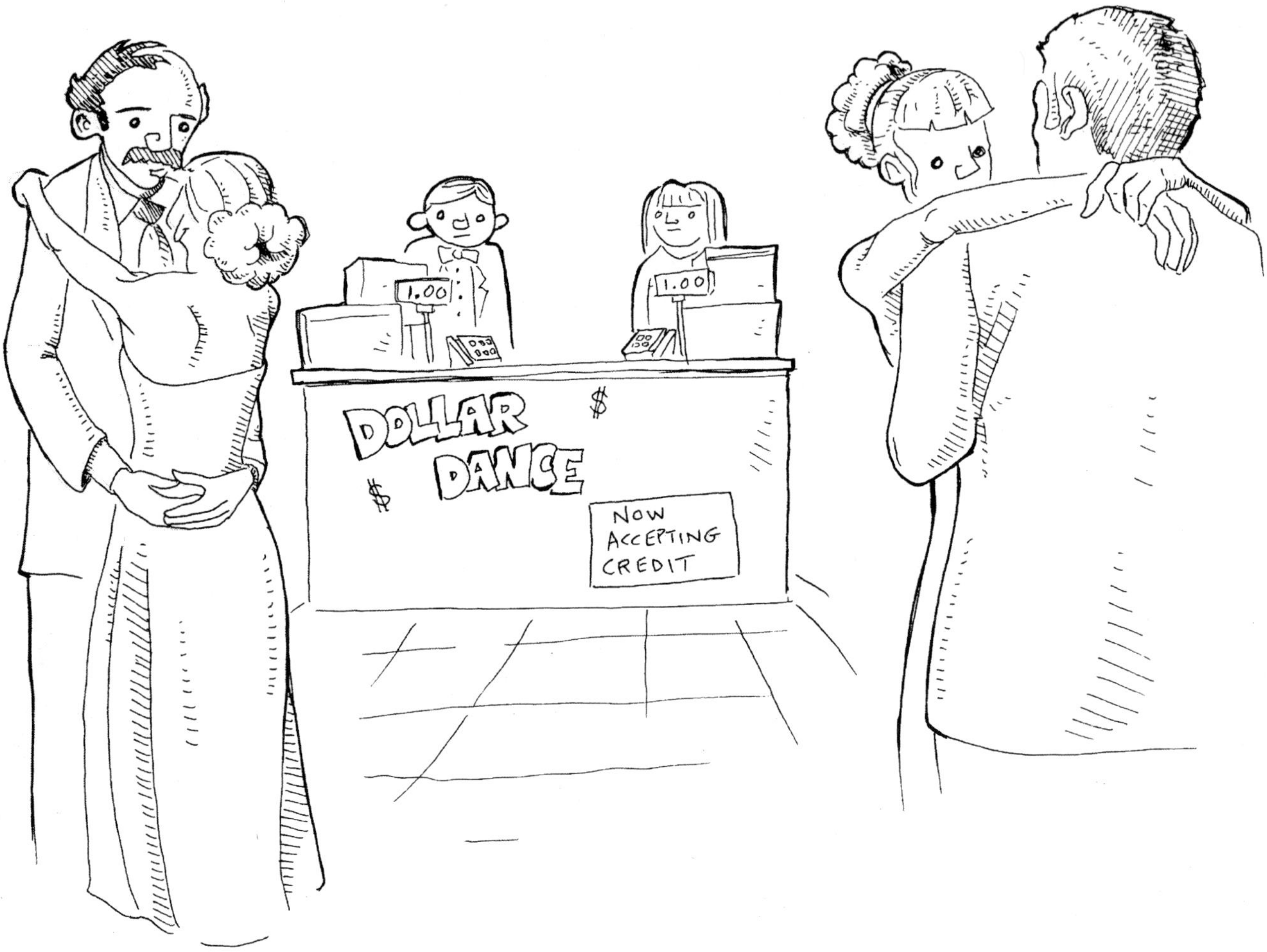
1.00
1.00
DOLLAR DANCE
NOW ACCEPTING CREDIT

98

DON'T have a dollar dance

The dollar dance is just a cheap, sleazy thing to do. We understand that you are going to need a lot of dollars to pay for your wedding, but maybe you should wait to start begging until after the night. Plus, the dollar dance breaks up the momentum of the evening, creating too many slow songs in a row—this is also widely known as a "buzz kill."

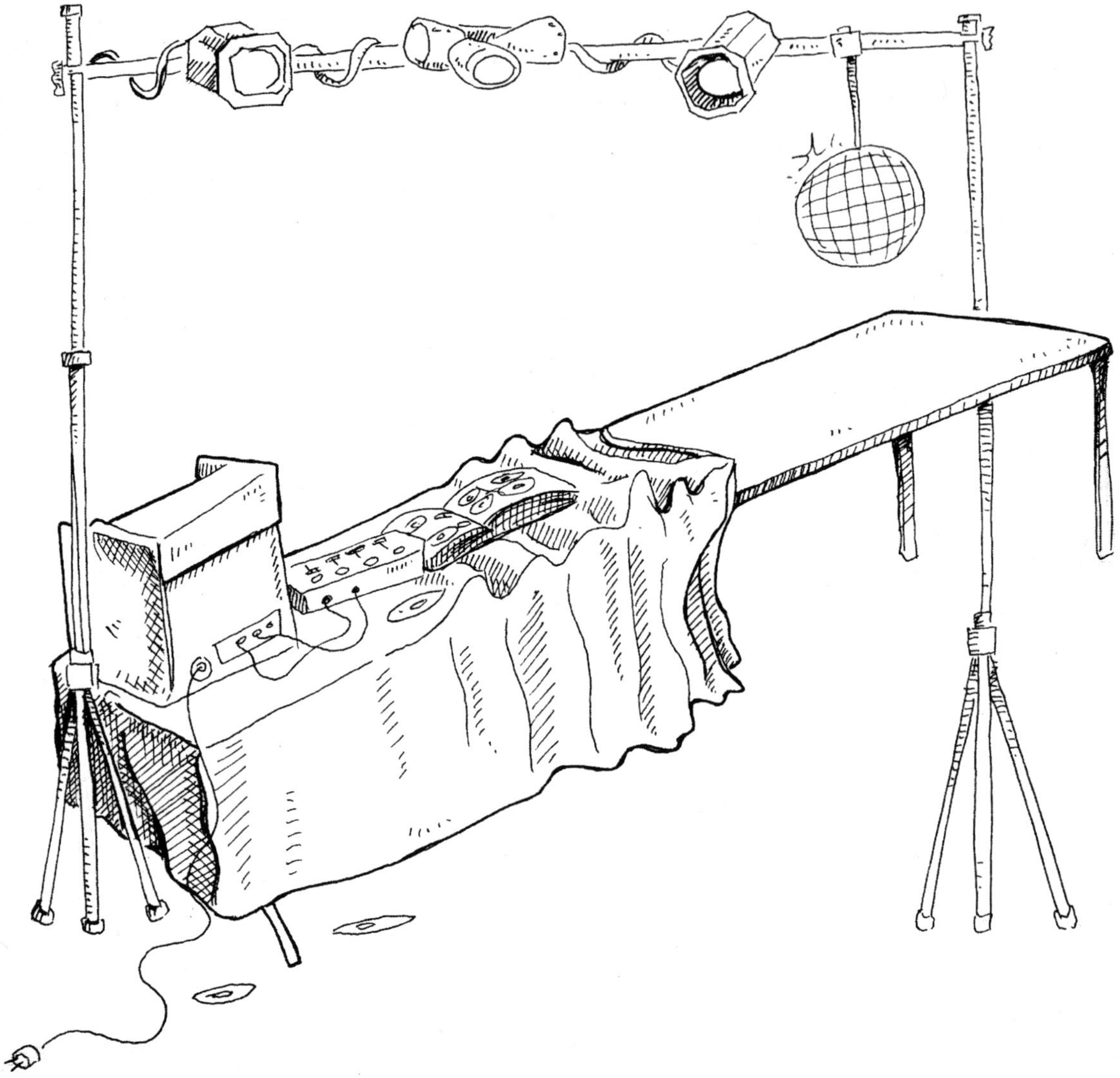

99

DON'T neglect your vendors' requirements

Your vendors have requirements for a reason. If your DJ asks for a 6' table and you get them an 8' table, then that might not work out very well. Just like you, your vendors have specific requirements for a reason. So, unless it sounds unreasonable, we suggest you provide what you promised your vendors so they can provide what they promised you.

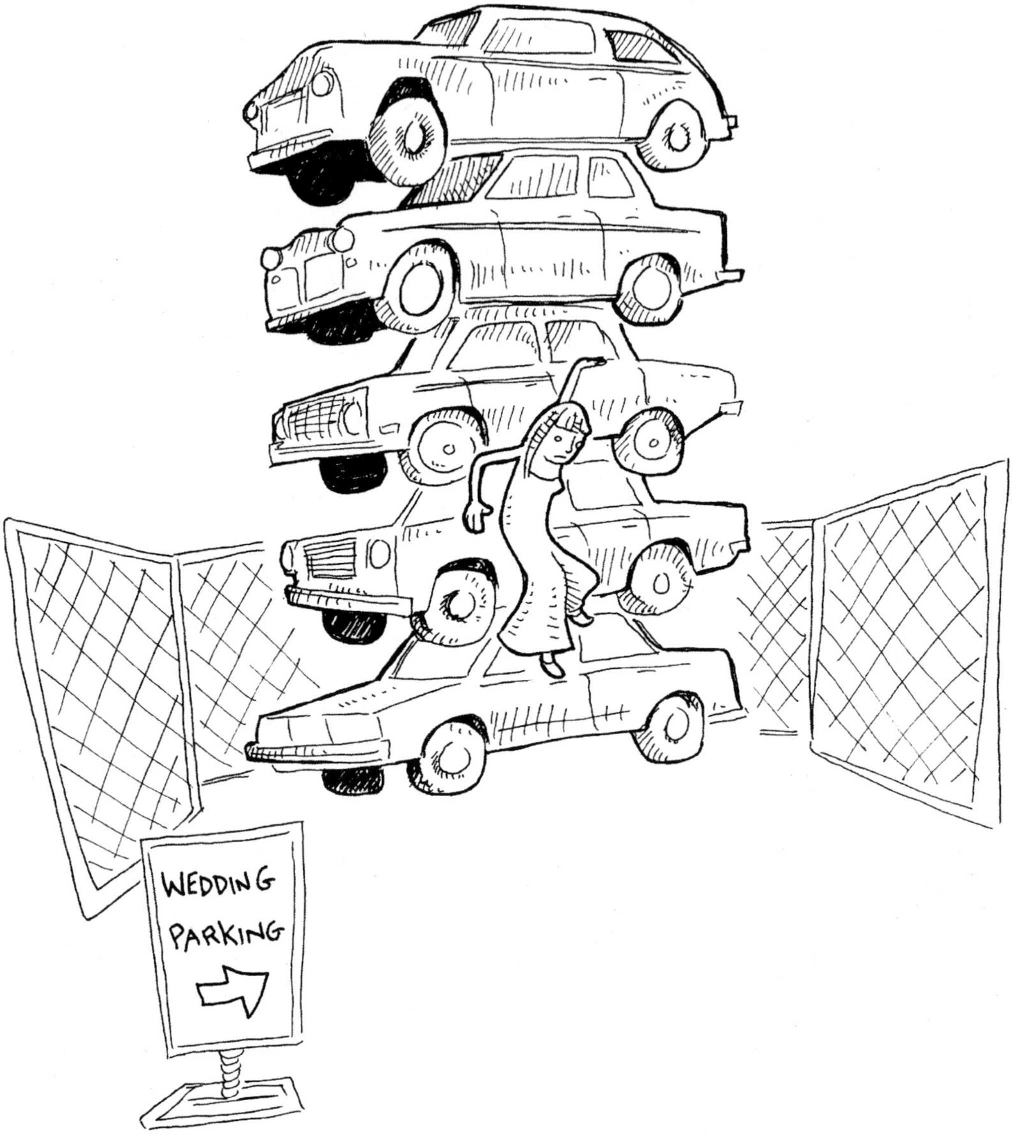
WEDDING
PARKING

100

DON'T select a location without ample parking

Where do you expect your guests to park if there is not enough parking?

101

DON'T forget to enjoy your wedding

We have talked a lot about what not to do through the course of this book—and we hope you have learned a few new things. Our biggest "DON'T" is to not forget to enjoy yourself. This can be the best day of your life as long as you take it with a grain of salt. Like every other day in your life, things will go wrong, and everything will not be perfect. But, in the end, if you are calm, relaxed, and just roll with the day no matter what happens, then you certainly will have a blast. Just smile and have fun with all of the people you care about—and those you probably would rather not see.

208

102

DON'T have caged exotic animals at your reception

OK, OK, fine—we actually could only come up with 101 good "DON'TS."

About the Authors

Greg Vass and Michael Kromm are co-owners of SolidLine Media, a High Definition video production company headquartered in downtown Chicago, Illinois. Mike Petrik heads up the SolidLine Art Department. You can learn more about SolidLine Media online at **www.solidlinemedia.com**.

Feel free to drop them an e-mail about anything but your complaints at the following addresses.

greg@weddingmishaps.com    **michael@weddingmishaps.com**    **mike@weddingmishaps.com**

Do you have a wedding "DON'T" or other funny wedding story you would like to share with us? Visit **www.weddingmishaps.com** and tell us about it.

102 DON'TS BEFORE YOU SAY "I Do"

THE SOMEWHAT COMPLETE
GUIDE TO
WEDDING MISHAPS

NEED MORE COPIES OF THE BOOK?
IT MAKES THE PERFECT GIFT (OR DRINK COASTER).

JUST VISIT US ONLINE AT WEDDINGMISHAPS.COM